Bujutsu Ha

A Quick Guide to Martial Arts

武術早學

Yamamoto Kansuke

Translation by Eric Shahan

ISBN: 978-1-950959-26-6

A Quick Guide to Martial Arts
A Closer Look at The Sword Scroll: Volume 3

Yamamoto Kansuke (1493-1561) was a hero of the century long Sengoku Era, roughly 1467-1600. Though partially blind and lame in one leg, Yamamoto Kansuke's prowess as a military strategist was legendary and his methods became a subject of study. In the Edo Era 1600-1868 several illustrated volumes attributed to him appeared, introducing his methods. These books explain his sword, spear and hidden weapon techniques.

The *A Closer Look at The Sword Scroll* series examines the many books attributed to Yamamoto Kansuke. While identical in parts, each book contains interesting variations that collectively add a great deal of information to those interested in traditional Japanese martial arts and military strategy. Originally presented as one volume, each book has been completely re-formatted and expanded, ideal for close study.

A Closer Look at The Sword Scroll volume 3 features *A Quick Guide to Martial Arts.* Both the date of publication and the artist are unclear, however it was probably published in the late Edo Era (19th century.) This version is notable since it includes two sections which are absent from volumes 1, 2 & 4. There is no table of contents in this volume, so I have titled them Unarmed Fighting and Staff Fighting. These two sections are unique to *A Quick Guide to Martial Arts.* However, they are identical to sections from a Chinese book compiled in 1621 called *Treatise on Armament Technology* by Mao Yuanyi. Further, the same Unarmed Fighting techniques are partially transcribed in a Meiji Era book called *Secrets of the Sword and Spear* by Ishibashi Nakawa. This information has all been included and translated.

Overview of *A Closer Look at the Sword Scroll* Volumes 1 ~4

Volume 1

軍法兵法記釼術之巻 Gunpo Hyohoki Kenjutsu no Maki (Published after 1546)

Way of the Sword and the Way of the Warrior: The Sword Scroll Gunpo Hyohoki Kenjutsu no Maki Zoho. Due to the opening remarks by Yamamoto Kansuke it was supposedly first published sometime after 1546.

Volume 2

剣道獨稽古 Kendo Hitori Geiko (19th century)

An Illustrated Guide to Kendo Solo Training is notable for its excellent illustrations of early Kendo armor as well as mysterious techniques to fight Tengu, mythical winged mountain goblins.

Volume 3

- **武術早學 Bujutsu Haya Manabi**
  A Quick Guide to Martial Arts
  19th Century
  This edition is notable for two additional sections showing boxing and wood staff techniques, which do not appear in any other version.

Volume 4

- **軍事参考軍法兵法記：楠正成秘書**
  Kusonogi Masashige Hissho Gunji Sanko Gunpo Heiho Ki
  Kusonogi Masashige's Secret Martial Arts Scroll on Military Strategy and Sword Fighting 1914
  This version contains commentary by researcher Wakichi Sakurai has a definitive publication date of. Sakurai draws parallels between Yamamoto Kansuke and the 14th century warlord Kusunoki Masashige 楠木正成 (1294 –1336.) He is held up as the ideal Samurai for his service to his lord.

Yamamoto Kansuke山本勘助

Yamamoto Kansuke getting his eye gouged out by a wild boar whilst hunting.
*Yamamoto Kansuke Gunpaiden*山本勘助軍配團 18th century

Yamamoto Kansuke (1493-1561) whose given name is variously written as 勘助、勘介 or 菅助 was born at the end of the late 15th or early 16th century and died at the fourth Kawanakajima battle in 1561. His woodpecker strategy, similar to the pincer movement, was widely praised as an example of excellent military tactics. Unfortunately he believed his woodpecker strategy to be a failure so he attempted to regain his honor by charging into the enemy ranks, being killed in action.

His military strategy was first recorded in a chapter of the *Koyo Gunkan*甲陽軍鑑 a 20 volume record of military strategy commissioned by the warlord Takeda Shingen. The oldest copy is from 1656.

Layout

Each page in this book has pictures of two combatants, as shown above. They are shown in different Stance, or stances, divided into three broad categories Jodan, Chudan and Gedan. Jodan is with the sword or spear held at or above head level, Chudan is around waist level and Gedan has the handle of the sword at waist level with the point facing the ground.

In addtion to the broad category of Jodan, Chudan and Gedan there is a sub-name for each illustration and a notation about foot positioning. The sub-names are quite poetic and therefore hard to translate accurately without being directly involved in this school of martial arts, therefore the translations should be considered approxamate. The notation regarding foot postitioning is either “floating foot” or “planted foot” which, based on the illustrations indicates the “ball of your foot off the ground” for the former and “foot flat on the ground” in the latter. It Some of the illustrations also contain additional information of varying lenghts.

For the most part each page will be presented as it was in the orininal book then each Stance will be isolated and enlarged, with the information on the page translated above. This is shown on the following page.

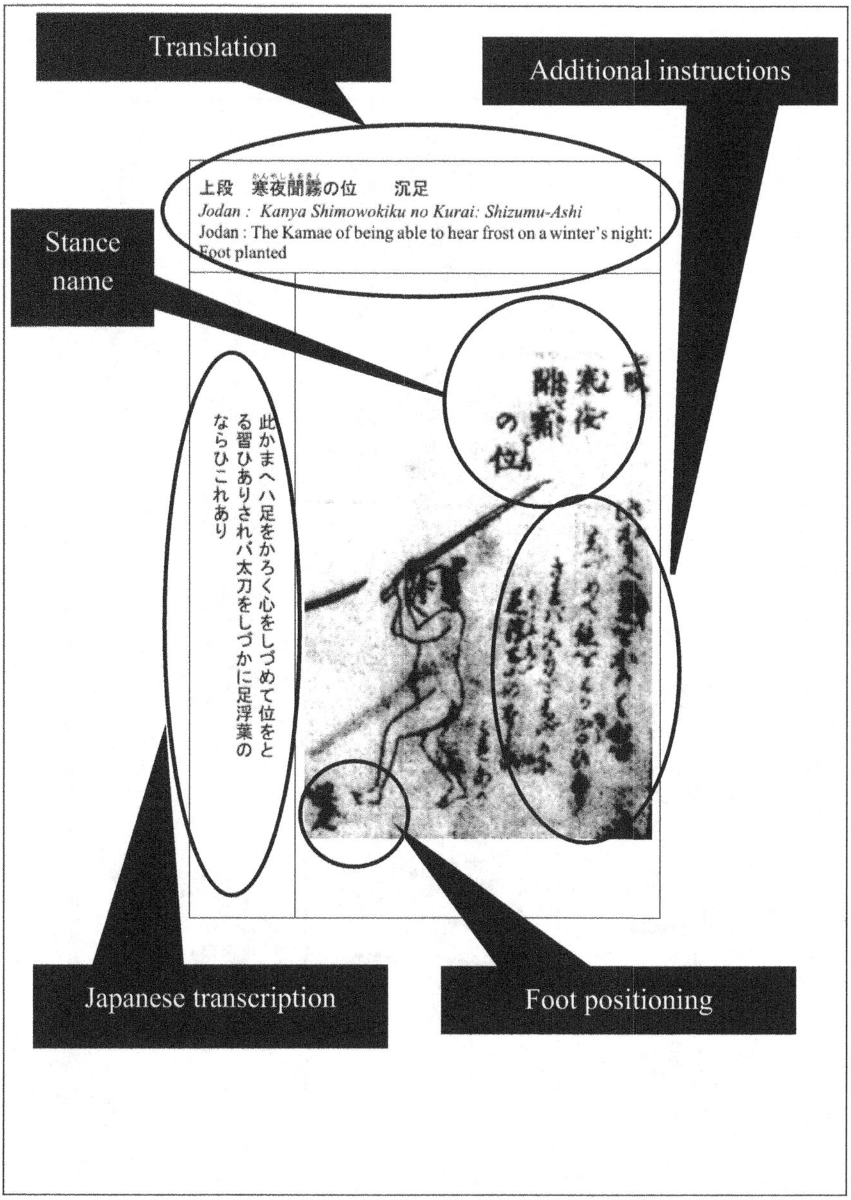
Translation
Additional instructions
上段　寒夜聞霜の位　　沈足
Jodan : Kanya Shimowokiku no Kurai: Shizumu-Ashi
Jodan : The Kamae of being able to hear frost on a winter's night: Foot planted
Stance name
此かまへハ足をかろく心をしづめて位をと
る習ひありされバ太刀をしづかに足浮葉の
ならひこれあり
Japanese transcription
Foot positioning

甲州住人　山本勘助著

武術早學

山家迺舍藏

Bujutsu Haya Manabi

A Quick Guide to Martial Arts

Resident of Koshu

Yamamoto Kansuke

Translated by Eric Shahan

Table of Contents

軍法兵法記飛術之巻

甲州住人　山本勘助著

飛術三ッの要をいふ事

夫飛術ニハ三ッの要あり 一ニハ心 二ニハ眼 三ニハ手足なり 此三ッのもの叶ざる時ハ勝道なる時ハ負るなり 心ニハ信りて眼動 眼ニ随て手足を動かせる事此心ニ従ふ 逆ニハ眼ニ手足さがるなど 手足眼心が合ふ時ハ其利なるんまで三ッのものおなじくして 慣れぬれ利ハ利あるべし 是迄の事ニ心眼手足の事を被成ゐきまず い人教がたし

上中下段構の事

是れ飛術構ゑる事 上段中段下段の三ッの形ハ第一是

甲州住人山本勘助

Record of Military Strategy and Soldiering: Kenjutsu Scroll

by Yamamoto Kansuke, Resident of Koshu

劔術三ツの要いふ事

The Three Essential Points of Kenjutsu

There are three basic principles in Kenjutsu. One is the spirit. The second is the eye. The third comprises the feet and hands. If these three are all in accordance/balance then you will achieve victory. If they are confused then you will be defeated. In accordance means that the spirit, the mind, is communicating to the eyes correctly. It means the eyes are correctly directing the feet and hands. In confusion means the eyes do not move in accordance with the spirit.

Having eyes delay the movement of the limbs of the body will give a poor result. However, if these three elements are activated correctly and in unison the result will be positive. This is exactly the same as the condition whereby having moved the hands you are not sure of where to put your feet.

細郷の地学なり文字と[illegible]る[illegible]自然[illegible]
わかつ[illegible]中小間細郷は[illegible]の[illegible]るべし[illegible]
[illegible]ありといふ[illegible] [illegible]て[illegible]
[illegible]この[illegible]をなる[illegible]て[illegible]その[illegible]
[illegible]故に[illegible]乃
[illegible]

撲は[illegible]太刀ものはこれなり又上段の内に上中下乃
三つの段をわかつ中段のも下段のもこの段にこれありて
[illegible]三十二あり 細郷は千変万化して[illegible]
[illegible]上中下の三段をなして[illegible]三段[illegible]
よく[illegible]て[illegible] 臨[illegible]変に応じて対する[illegible]要也

上中下段構の事
Jodan, Chudan and Gedan Stances

When going into stances with a sword, know that Jodan, Chudan and Gedan are the only Kamae. This is the first lesson of Kenjutsu. Further, when studying and adapting your body to these Kamae having Yokoshimana Kokoro 邪な心 or no evil in your heart is best.

A person came to me once and said "In Kenjutsu the shape changes depending on the enemy. It follows then that there is only one Kimeru 極める, or only one rule, in Kenjutsu. What do you think of this?

The response was, "Having control over your spirit is certainly a Kimeru 極める. And having learned the three principals, or Kaname 要, you can consider yourself to have arrived, or Itaru 至る. Having achieved this state of Shigoku 至極, or the ultimate, there is really nothing more to be said. For that reason, the way in which the arms and legs are bent should be studied extensively.

For example, this applies in the same way to both Yari and Naginata. Further, within Jodan Kamae there lies Jo-upper, Chu-middle and Ge-lower. Also within Chudan Kamae there lies Jo-upper, Chu-middle and Ge-lower. All together there are thirty-three versions. It is said that Kenjutsu contains Sen-pen-ban-ka 千変万化 or a thousand changes and ten thousand variations, or Muryo or without end. However there are no other Kamae than Jodan, Chudan and Gedan. Those that are Shoshin Sha or beginners should study these three levels. Taking hold of any chance and responding to any Henka, or variation, by striking is of the upmost importance.

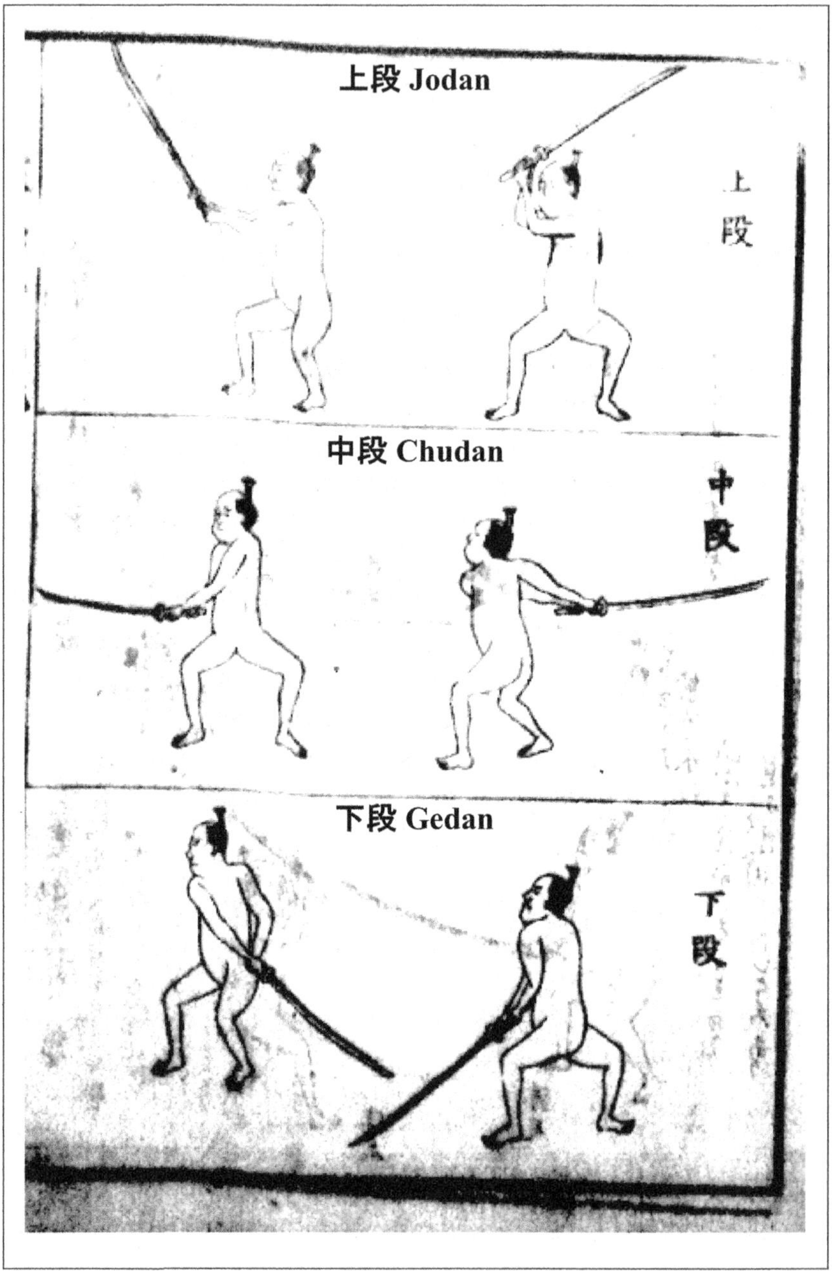
上段 Jodan
上段
中段 Chudan
中段
下段 Gedan
下段

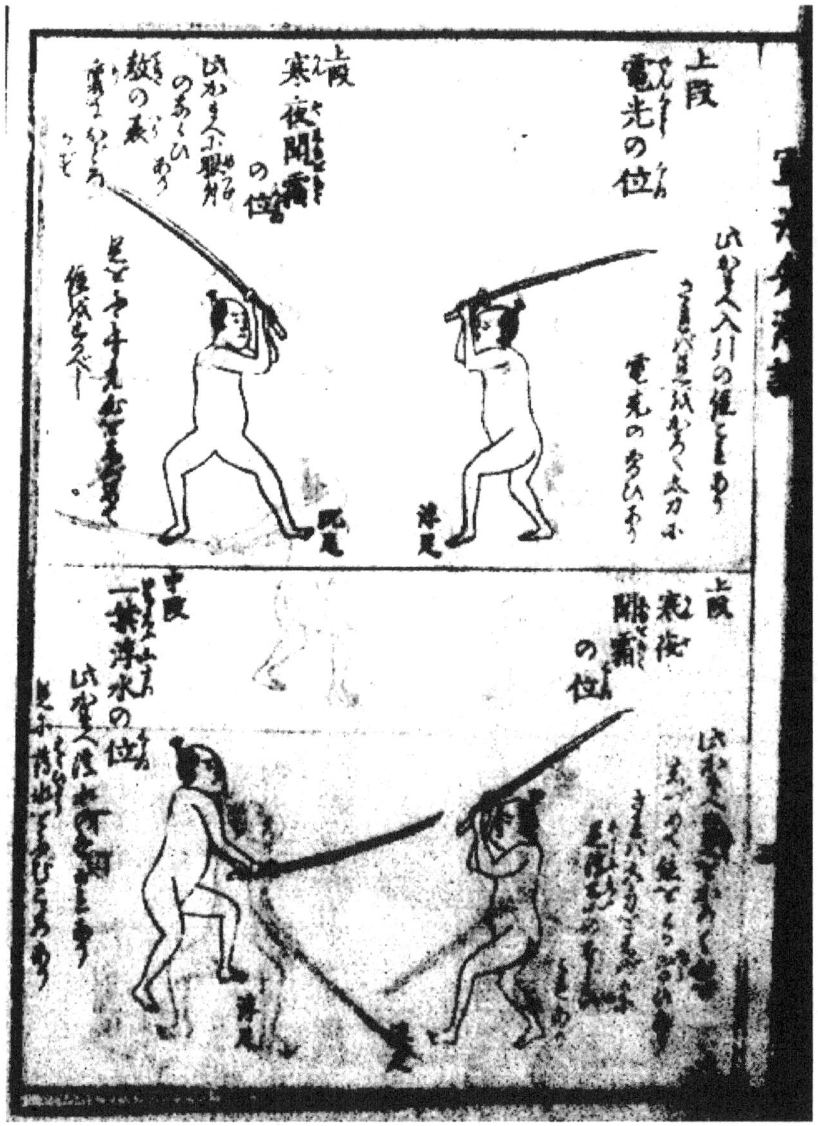
上段
電光の位
上段
寒夜聞霜の位
中段
一葉浮水の位

上段の位　浮足

Jodan : Denko no Kurai : Uki-ashi

Jodan : Lightning Stance : Floating foot

This Kamae is about the Ma-ai 間合い or distancing of Irimi 入身, or entering into an ideal space in response to the opponent's attack or movement, and Hikimi 引身, or drawing back into an ideal position in response to the opponent's attack or movement. The foot is lightly touching the ground, the Tachi 太刀 is imbibed with the Denko Hiden, or the secret teaching of lightning.

上段の位　浮足

此かまえ入引の位これありされバ足をかろく、太刀に電光の習ひあり

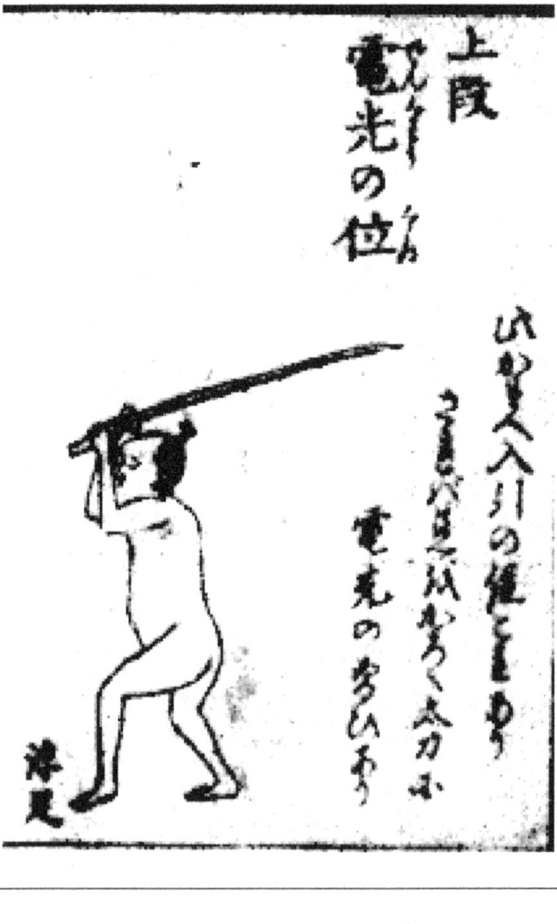

<table>
<tr><td colspan="2">上段　Error!の位　　沉足
Jodan : Kanya Shimowokiku no Kurai: Shizumu-Ashi
Jodan : The Kamae of being able to hear frost on a winter's night: Foot planted</td></tr>
<tr><td>此かまへハ足をかろく心をしづめて位をとる習ひありされバ太刀をしづかに足浮葉のならひこれあり</td><td></td></tr>
</table>

上段　Error!の位　浮足

Jodan : Kanya Shimowokiku no Kurai: Shizumu-Ashi

Jodan : The stance of being able to hear frost crack on a winter's night : Floating foot

The secret teaching of this stance is to stay light on your feet and calm your spirit. Having done that draw the Tachi and position it silently. The feet should be kept as light as a leaf floating on water. The feet are of upmost importance.

此かまへに眼付けのならひあり敵
の表裏におどろかず足をふみすゑ
心をしづめて位をとるべし

中段　の位　沉足

Chudan : Ichi-e Fusui no Kurai : Shizumu-Ashi

Chudan : Leaf floating upon water Stance: Foot Planted

The meaning of this stance is to position yourself like a leaf floating upon water. The feeling should be as if the feet are stepping on ice.

此かまへ浮水の習これあり足にError!を
ふむこゝろあり

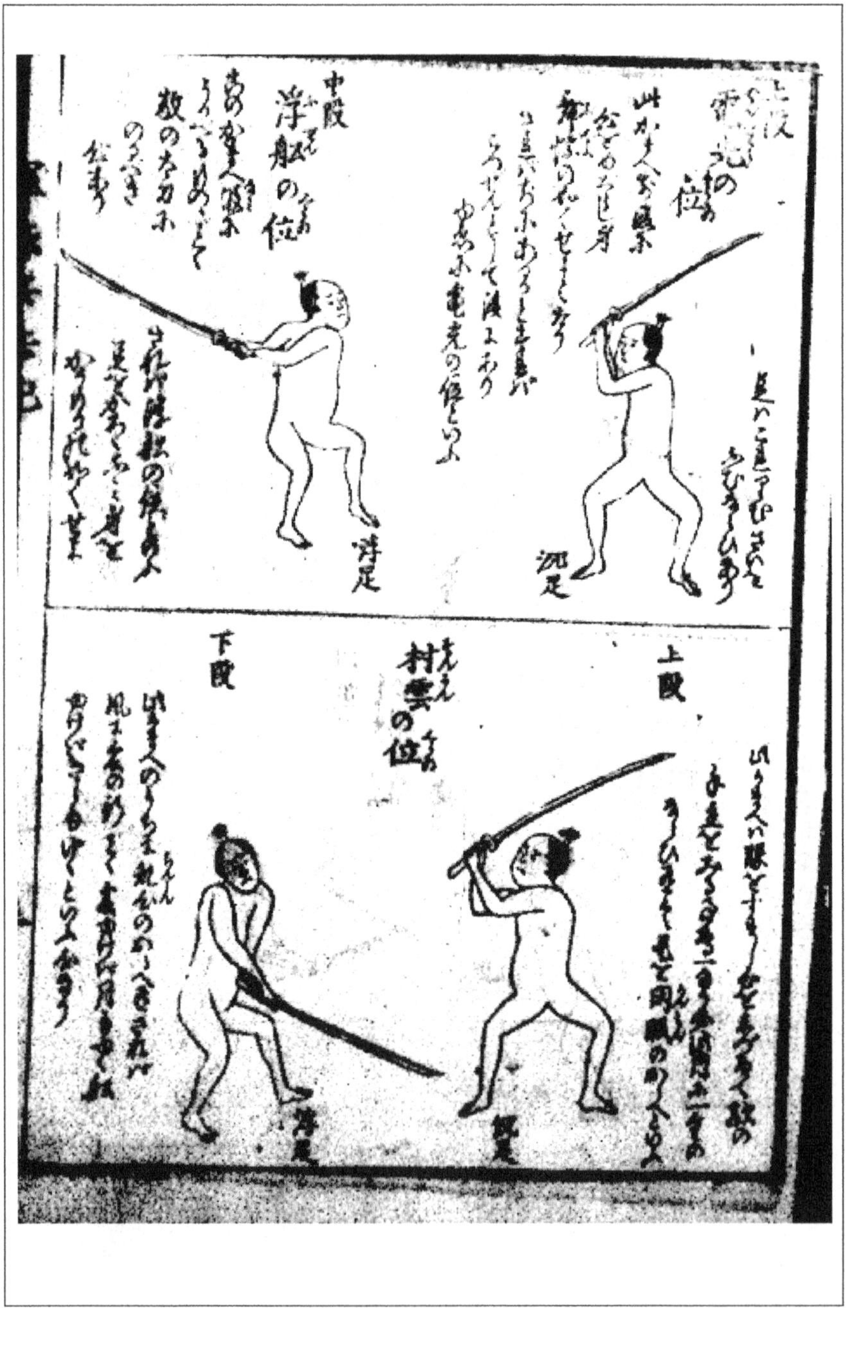
中段
浮舩の位
上段
村雲の位
下段

電光の位　沈足

Jodan : Denko no Kurai : Shizumu-Ashi

Jodan : Lightning Stance : Foot Planted

As you alternate switching your feet out your center of gravity moves back to front. For this stance you should concentrate on both what is in front of you as well as what is behind you. Your body should move lightly, dancing like a butterfly. If done in this fashion, from the opponent's point of view, it will seem to him as if you are in front of him when suddenly you have circled around behind him. Therefore you are extremely hard to corner. This is the stance known as Denko no Kurai, the Lightning Stance.

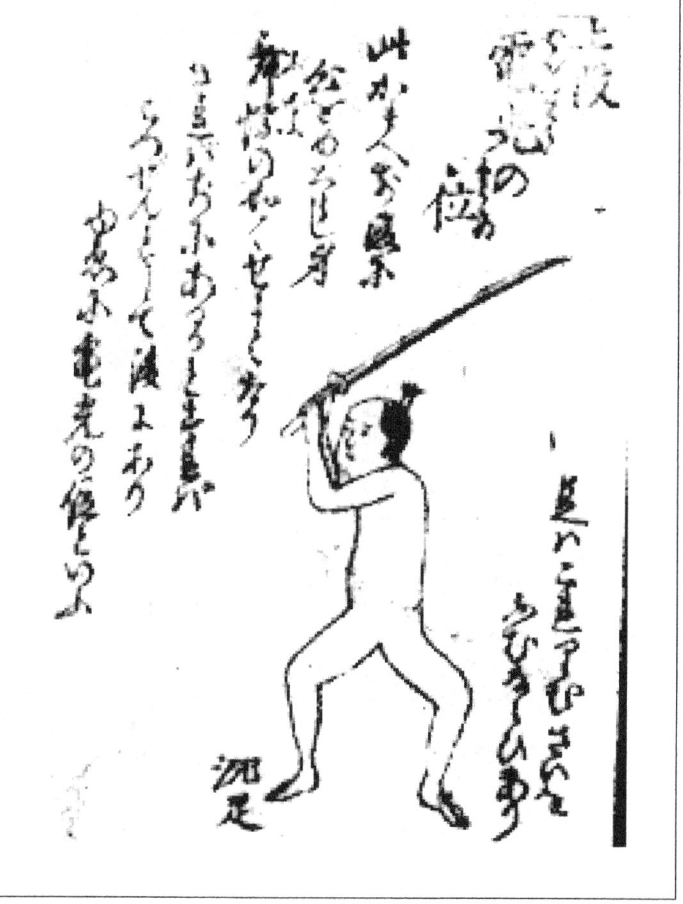

此かまへ前後に心をめぐらし身舞蝶の如くせよとなり
されば前にあるかとすればこつぜんとして後にあり
ゆえに電光の位といふ足ハこれりむさいをふむならひあり

中段　Error!の位　浮足

Chudan Fusen no Kurai : Uki-Ashi

Chudan : The Floating Boat Stance : Floating Foot.

The feeling of this stance is of watching the opponent's Tachi while you float like an object going up and down waves. That is why this Stance is called Fusen no Kurai, the Floating Boat Stance. The feet are touching lightly and the bodyweight should be placed as lightly as a feather.

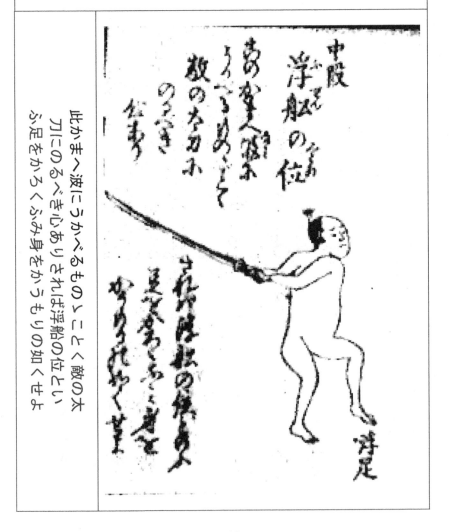

此かまへ波にうかべるものゝごとく敵の太刀にのるべき心ありされば浮船の位といふ足をかろくふみ身をかうもりの如くせよ

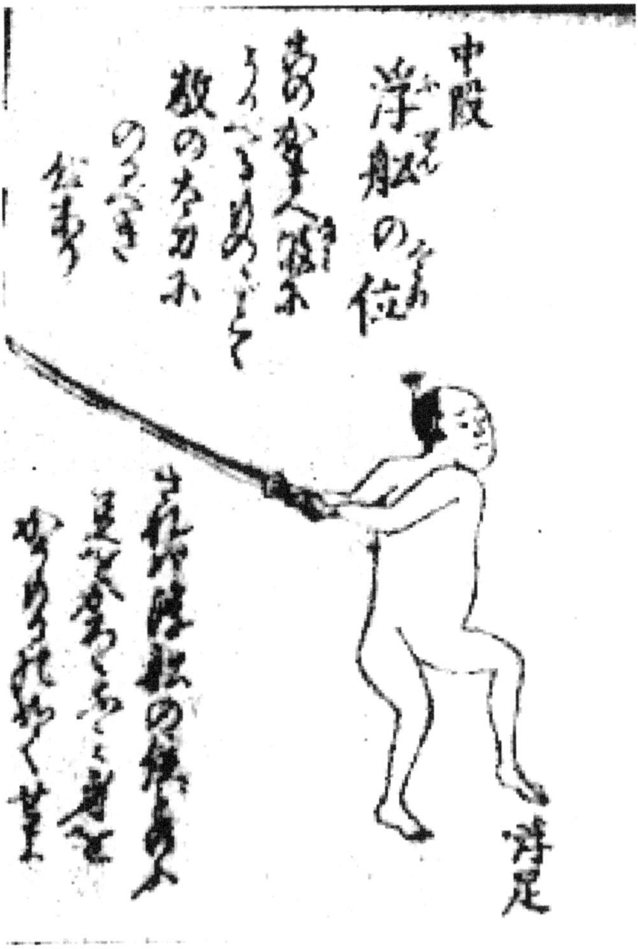

上段　村雲の位　沉足

Jodan : Sonun no Kurai : Shizumu-Ashi

Jodan : Cloudy Village Stance : Planted foot

Keep the feet together and impart a sense of sleepiness. The meaning of this stance is to clear your vision, calm your spirit and focus everything on the opponent's strategy. By doing this you will invariably discern something.

此かまへハ眼をすまし心をしづめて敵の手位をみる事専一なり、必此内に一重のならひ有之是を開眼のおしへといふ

下段 村雲の位　浮足

Gedan : Sonun no Kurai : Uki-Ashi

Gedan : Cloudy Village Stance : Floating Foot

There is nothing in this stance that teaches that the spirit is in tumult. Like windblown clouds, across the face of the moon your spirit should be like a boat slowly being swept up onto the beach.

Note: The Kanji for Cloudy Village Stance are sometimes written as Sonun no Kurai and sometimes as Murakumo.

此かまへのうちに乱心のおしへ有、されバ風に雲の行ごとく雲ゆけば月もゆく船ゆけばきしもゆくといふ心なり

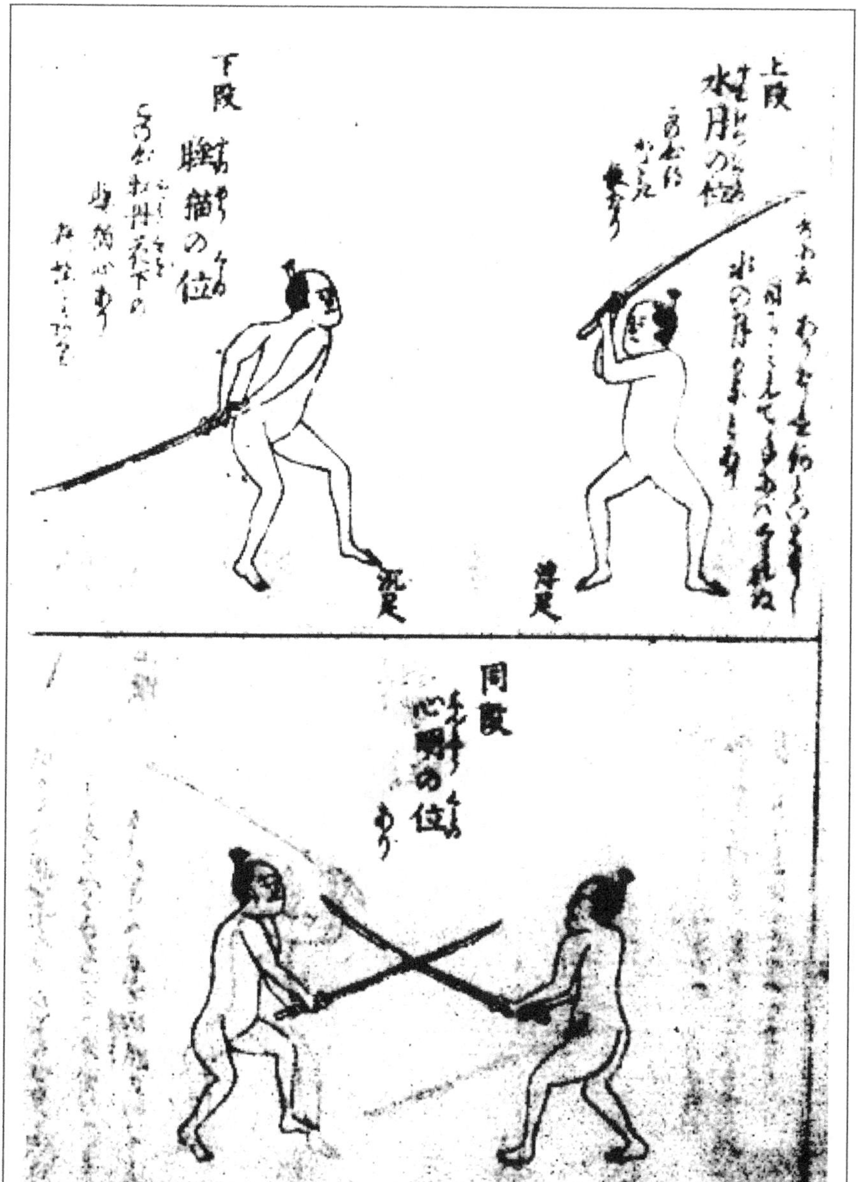
上段
水月の位
下段
同段
心明の位

上段　水月の位　浮足

Jodan : Suigetsu no Kurai : Uki-Ashi

Jodan : Moon Reflected on Water Stance : Floating Foot

There is a song that talks of how this is a difficult stance to adopt. It is said that what is there is not there. The water that pools in one hand shows a different moon from the one above.

この心得かたき位なり歌に云う、ありなしを何といはまし月にミえて手にハしられぬ水の月かなとあり

下段　Error!の位　沉足

Gedan : Suibyou no Kurai : Shizumu-Ashi

Gedan : Sleeping Cat Stance : Planted Foot

The way of thinking about this stance is a sleeping cat below a Botan flower with a dancing butterfly above.

この心Error!の睡猫心あり舞蝶とあり

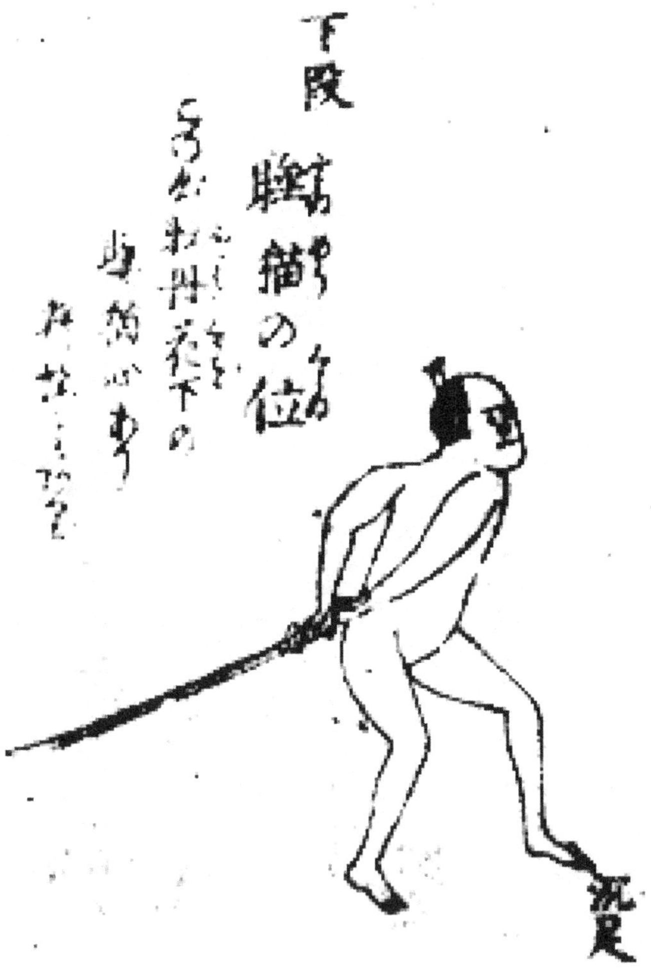

同段　　心妙の位あり
Do-Stance : Shinmyo no Kurai
Same Stance: Mysterious Heart Stance

There is a Kuden, Orally Transmitted Lesson

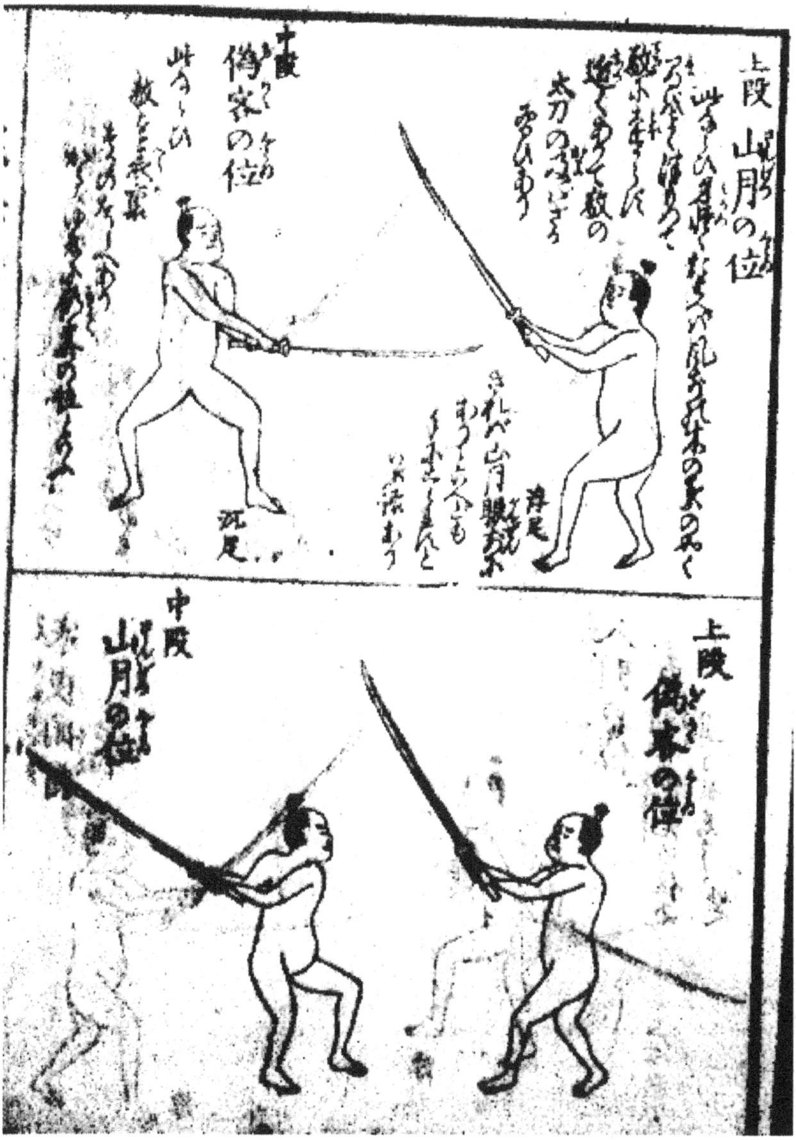
上段
山月の位
中段
中段
上段

上段　山月の位　浮足

Jodan : Sangetsu no Kurai : Uki-Ashi

Jodan : Mountain Moon Stance : Floating Foot

For this Stance you should hold your body as light as a leaf on a tree being brushed by the wind. Maintain your Ma-ai, or distance, but do not allow the enemy too much space. Maintain a close distance but out of range of the enemy's Tachi. The meaning of this Stance is that while you can see mountains or the moon with your eyes you are unable to take them into your hand.

此ならひ身軽くたとへバ風前の木の葉の如く。間をよく
つもつて敵にからすくありて敵の太刀の及バざる習ひあり
されバ山月眼前にありといへども手にしられずといふ語あり

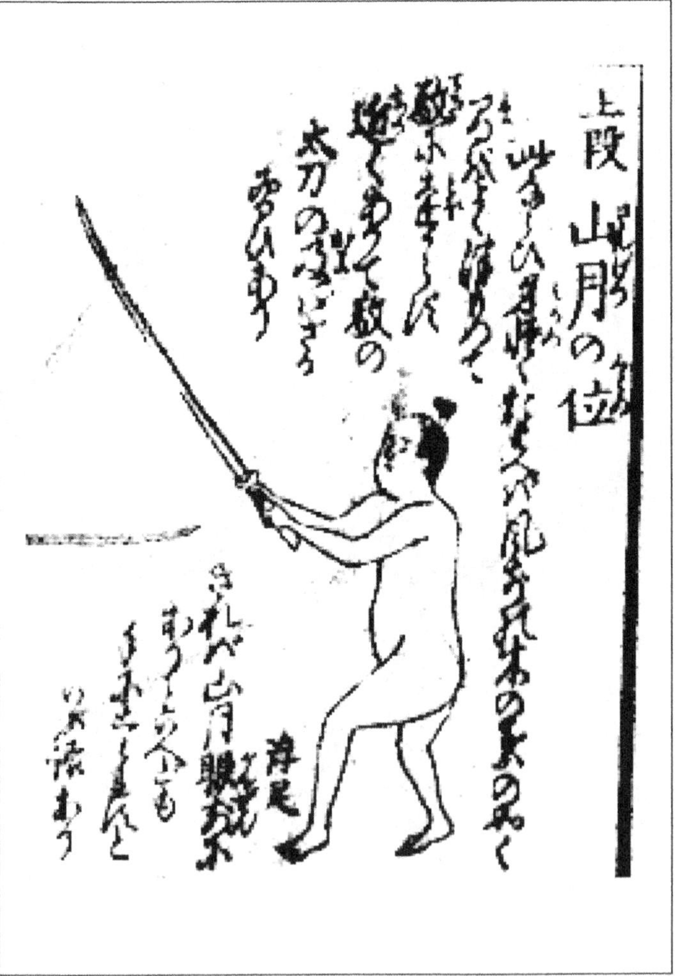

中段　偽客の位　　沉足

Chudan : Gikaku no Kurai : Shizumu Ashi

Chudan : False Guest Stance : Planted Foot

This Stance contains teachings on how to control the Hyori, or Obverse and Reverse, of the opponent. Both his true and hidden intent. For that reason it is known as Gikaku, False Guest.

此ならひ敵を表裏するのをしへありかるがゆえに偽客のくらいといふ

(Left) 中段山月の位 Chudan : *Sangetsu no Kurai*
Chudan : Mountain Moon Stance

(Right) 上段偽客の位 *Jodan* : *Gikaku no Kurai*
Jodan : False Guest Stance

上段
清眼の位
下段
入引の位

上段　清眼の位　浮足

Jodan Seigan no Kurai Uki-Ashi

Jodan : Seigan Stance: Floating foot

Here you are meant to keep your eye on the end of the opponent's Tachi while at the same time keep your other eye on the eight directions around you.

眼を敵の太刀先につけ八面一眼といふ習あり
ことわりまへにあり

下段　の位　沉足

Gedan Suibyo no Kurai Shizumu-Ashi

Gedan: Sleeping Cat Stance : Planted foot

Explanation is the same as before

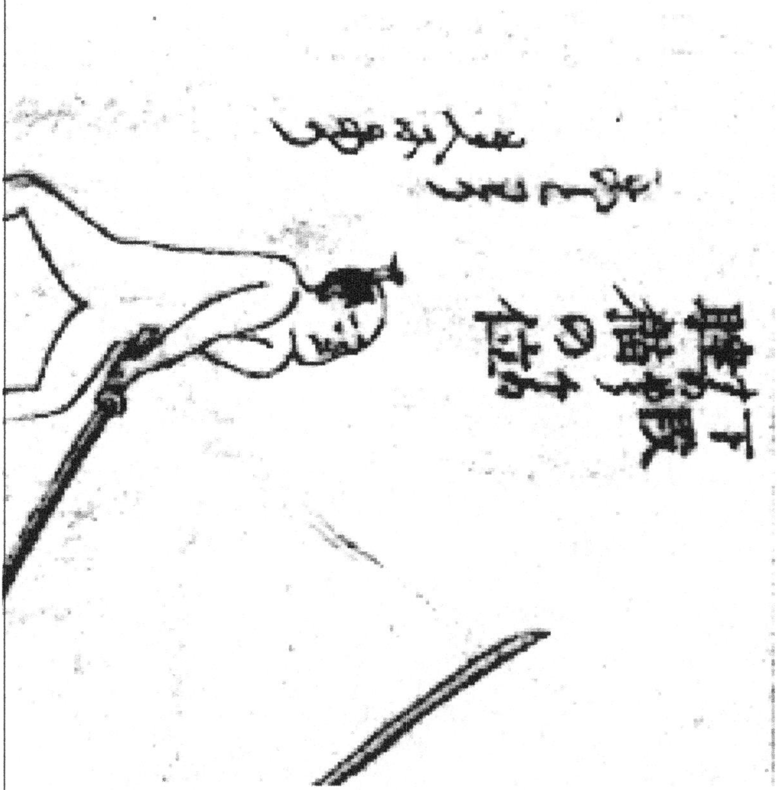

の位　浮

Kanyashimo wo Kiku no Kurai Uki-Ashi

Floating foot : The stance of being able to hear frost crack on a winter's night : Floating Foot.

Note: I presume this is Jodan, however there is no notation.

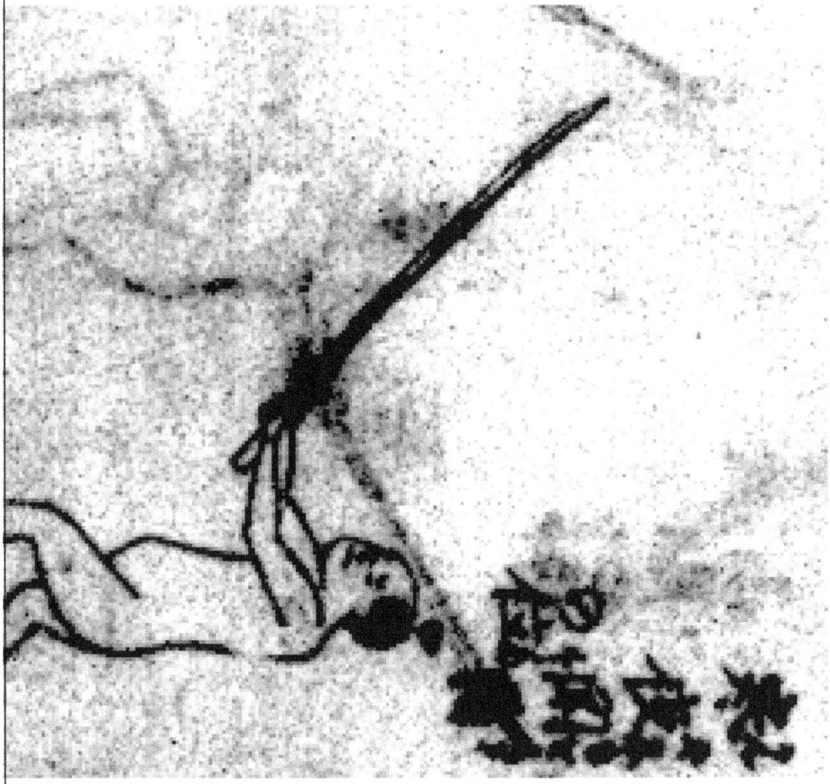

入引の位　浮
ことわり電光の位にに書くしるし候也
Nyuin no Kurai Uki-Ashi
Moving In and Out Stance : Floating Foot

The explanation for this is the same as for Denko no Kurai.

Note: I presume this is Gedan, however there is no notation.

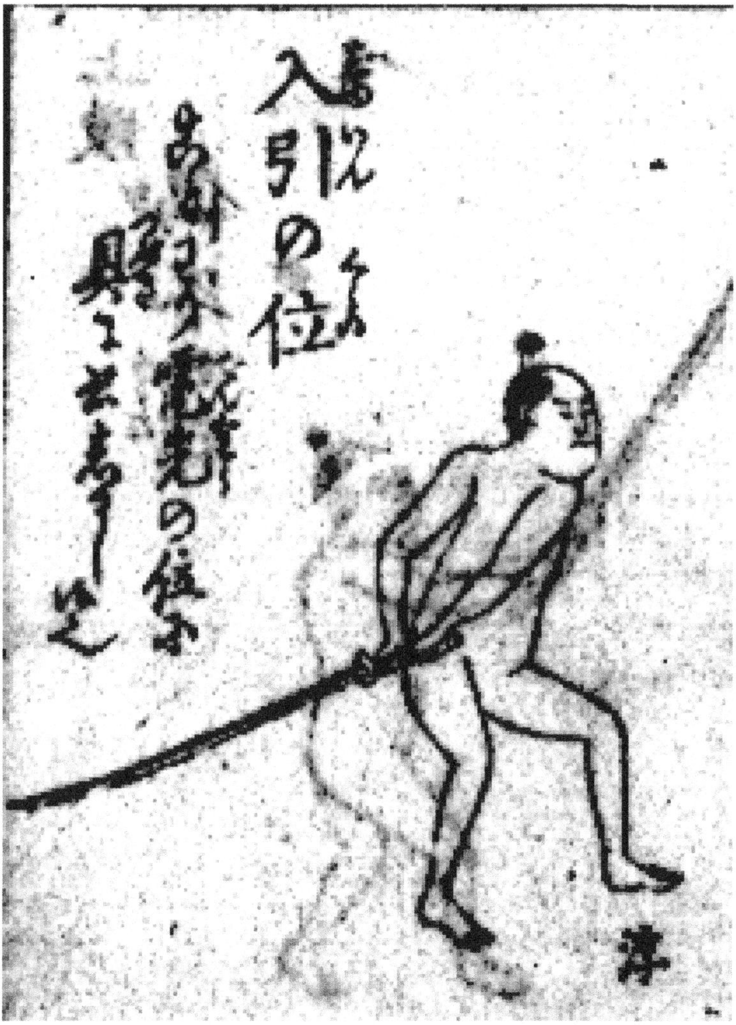

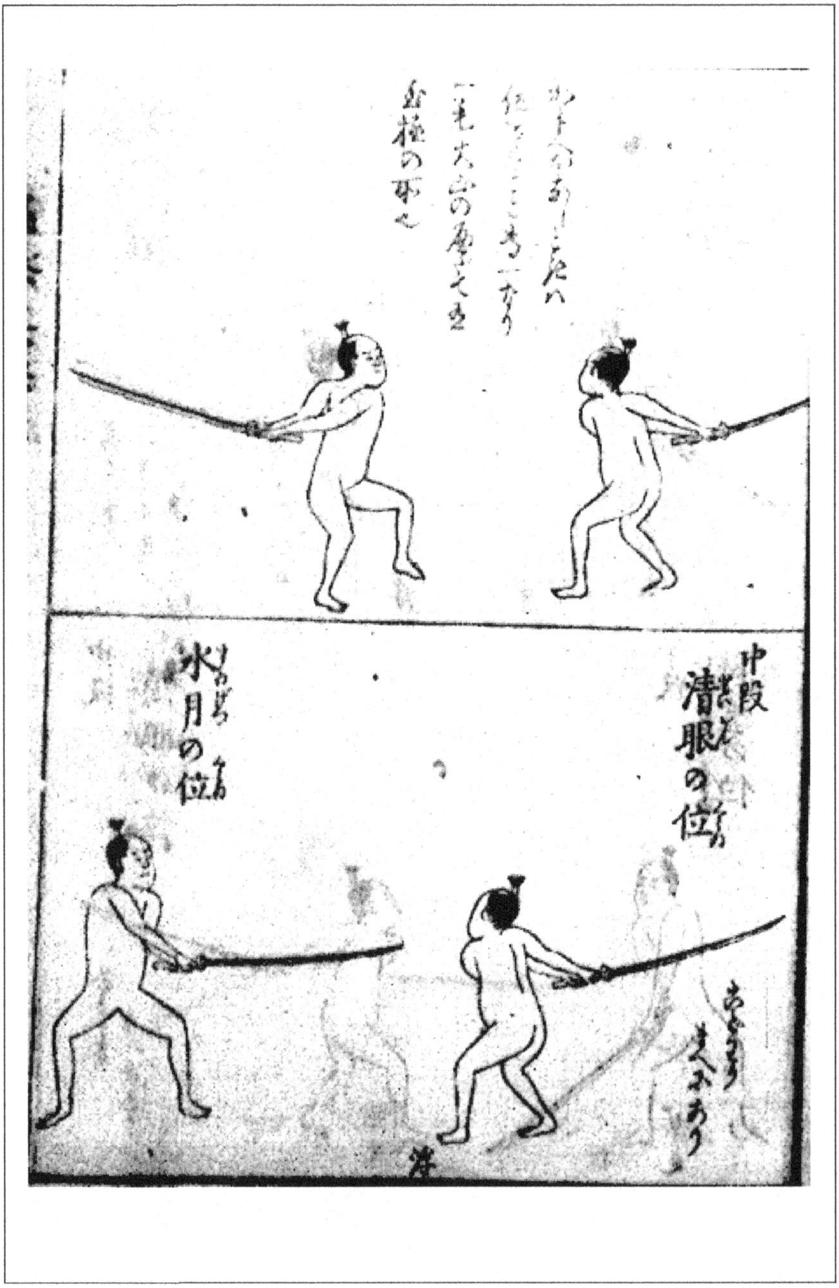
中段
清眼の位
水月の位

(Right) 中段 清眼の位 浮 *Chudan : Seigan no Kurai : Uki-Ashi*
Chudan : Clear-eyed Stance : Floating foot
ことわりまへにあ Explanation is as before.

(Left) 下段 村雲の位 浮 *Gedan : Murakumo no Kurai : Uki-Ashi* Gedan: Cloudy Village Stance : Floating foot

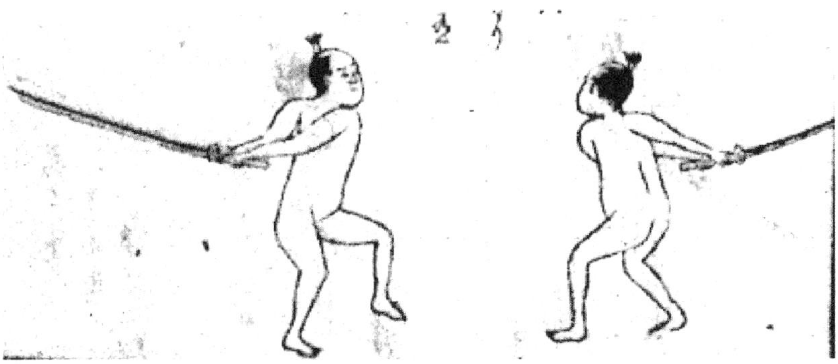

(Right) 中段清眼の位浮足 *Chudan : Seigan no Kurai : Uki-Ashi* Chudan : Clear-eyed Stance : Floating foot
ことわりまへにあり Explanation is as before.

(Left) 下段　村雲の位 Gedan : Murakumo no Kurai
Gedan :

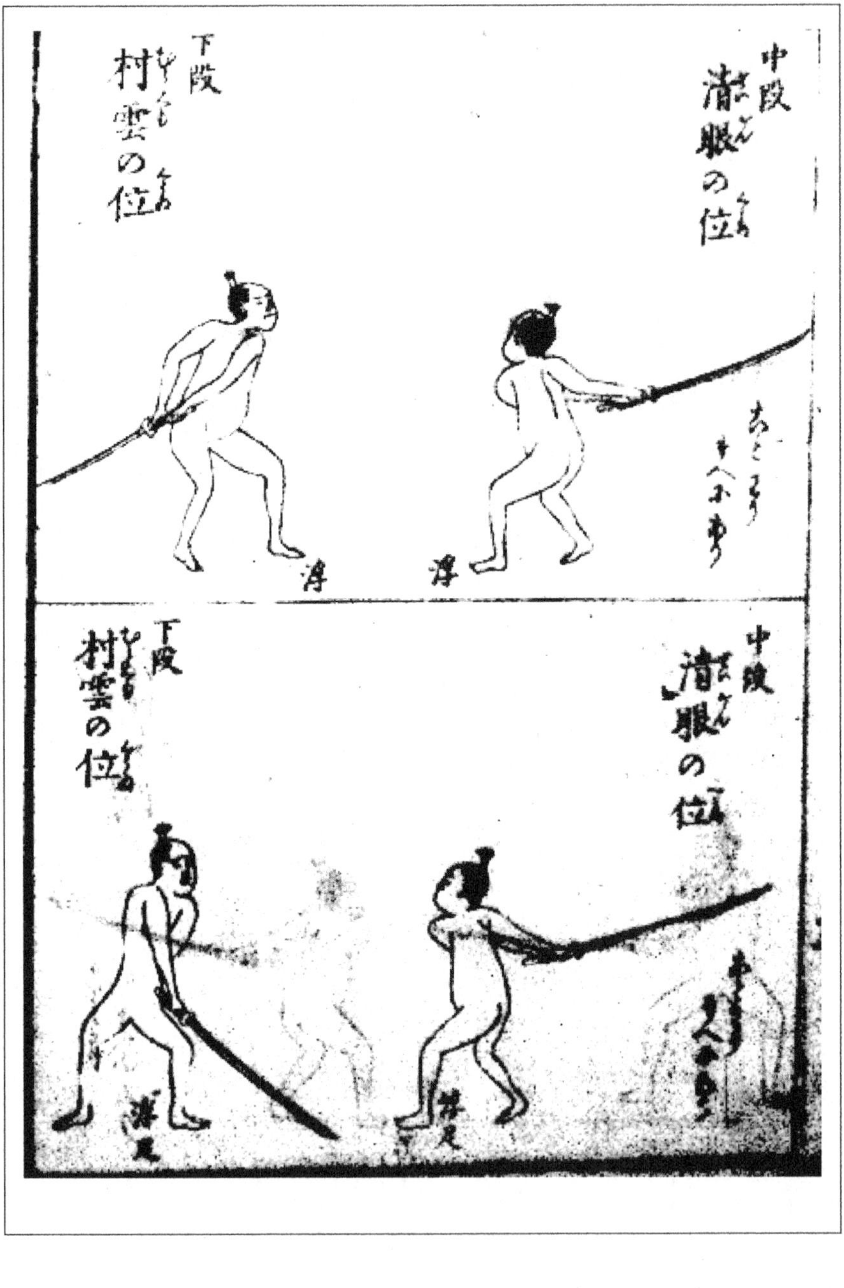
中段
清眼の位
下段
村雲の位
中段
清眼の位
下段
村雲の位

(Right) 中段 清眼の位 浮 *Chudan : Seigan no Kurai : Uki-Ashi* Chudan : Clear-eyed Stance : Floating foot
ことわりまへにあ Explanation is as before.

(Left) 下段 村雲の位 浮 *Gedan : Murakumo no Kurai : Uki-Ashi* Gedan: Cloudy Village Stance : Floating foot

(Right) 中段清眼の位浮足 *Chudan : Seigan no Kurai : Uki-Ashi* Chudan : Clear-eyed Stance : Floating foot
ことわりまへにあり Explanation is as before.

(Left) 下段 村雲の位 Gedan : Murakumo no Kurai
Gedan :

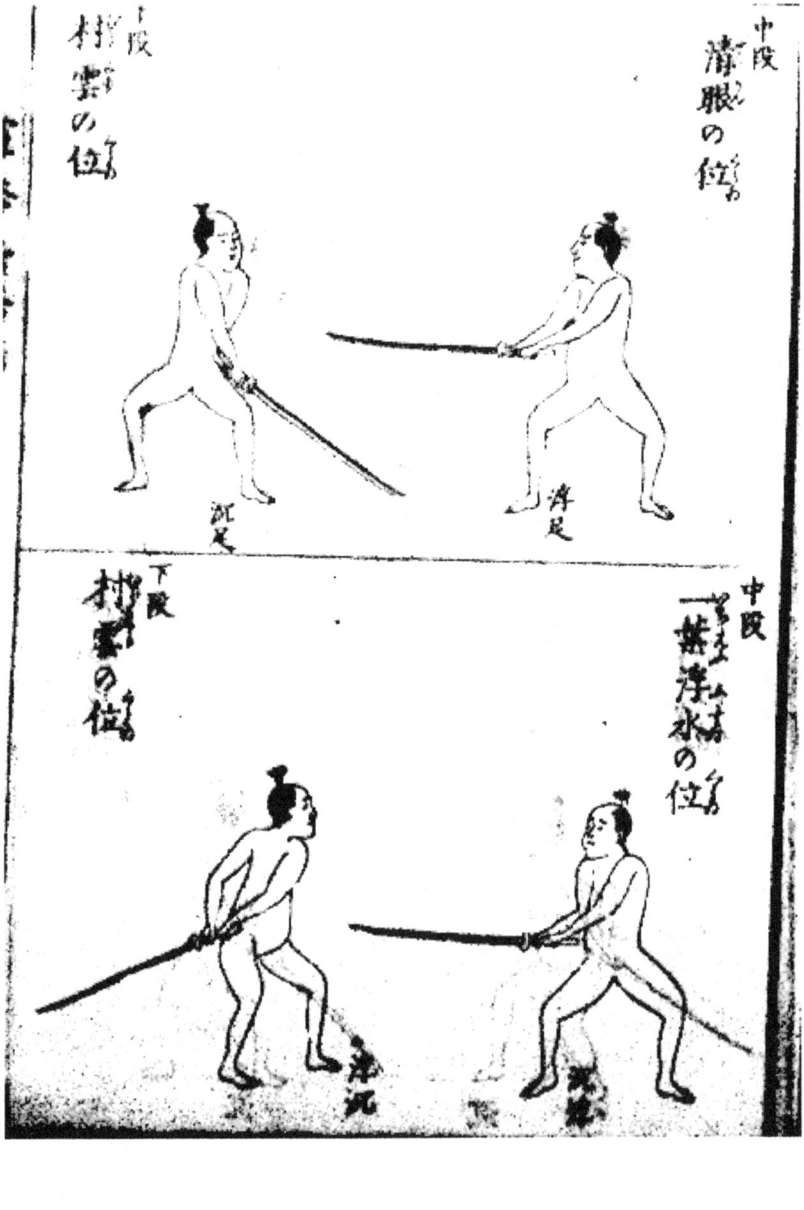
中段
清眼の位
下段
中段
一葉浮水の位
下段

(Right)
中段　清眼の位浮足 *Chudan : Seigan no Kurai : Uki-Ashi*
Chudan : Clear-eyed Stance : Floating foot

(Left)
下段 村雲の位沉 *Gedan : Murakumo no Kurai :Shizumu-Ashi*
Gedan : Cloudy Village Stance : Planted foot

(Right)
中段 清眼の位沉 *Chudan : Seigan no Kurai : Shizumu-Ashi*
Chudan : Clear-eyed Stance : Planted Foot

(Left)
下段　村雲の位浮足 *Gedan : Murakumo no Kurai : Uki-Ashi*
Gedan : Cloudy Village Stance : Floating Foot

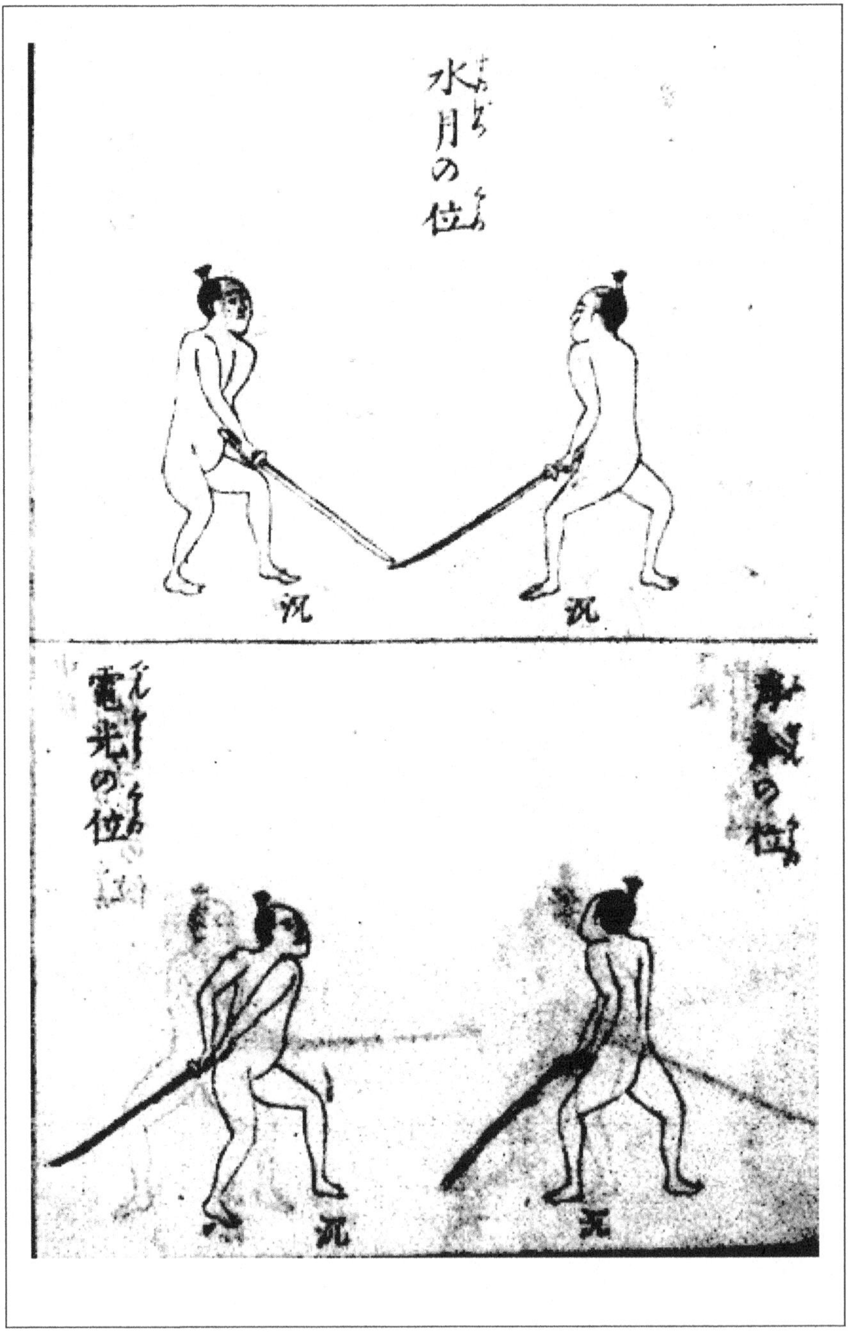
水月の位
電光の位

水月の位沈足 *Suigetsu no Kurai : Shizumu-Ashi*
Clear-eyed Stance : Planted Foot

(Left)
電光の位沉足 *Denko no Kurai : Shizumu-Ashi*
Lightning Bolt Stance : Planted Foot

(Right)
の位沉足 *Fusen no Kurai : Shizumu-Ashi*
Floating Boat Stance : Planted Foot

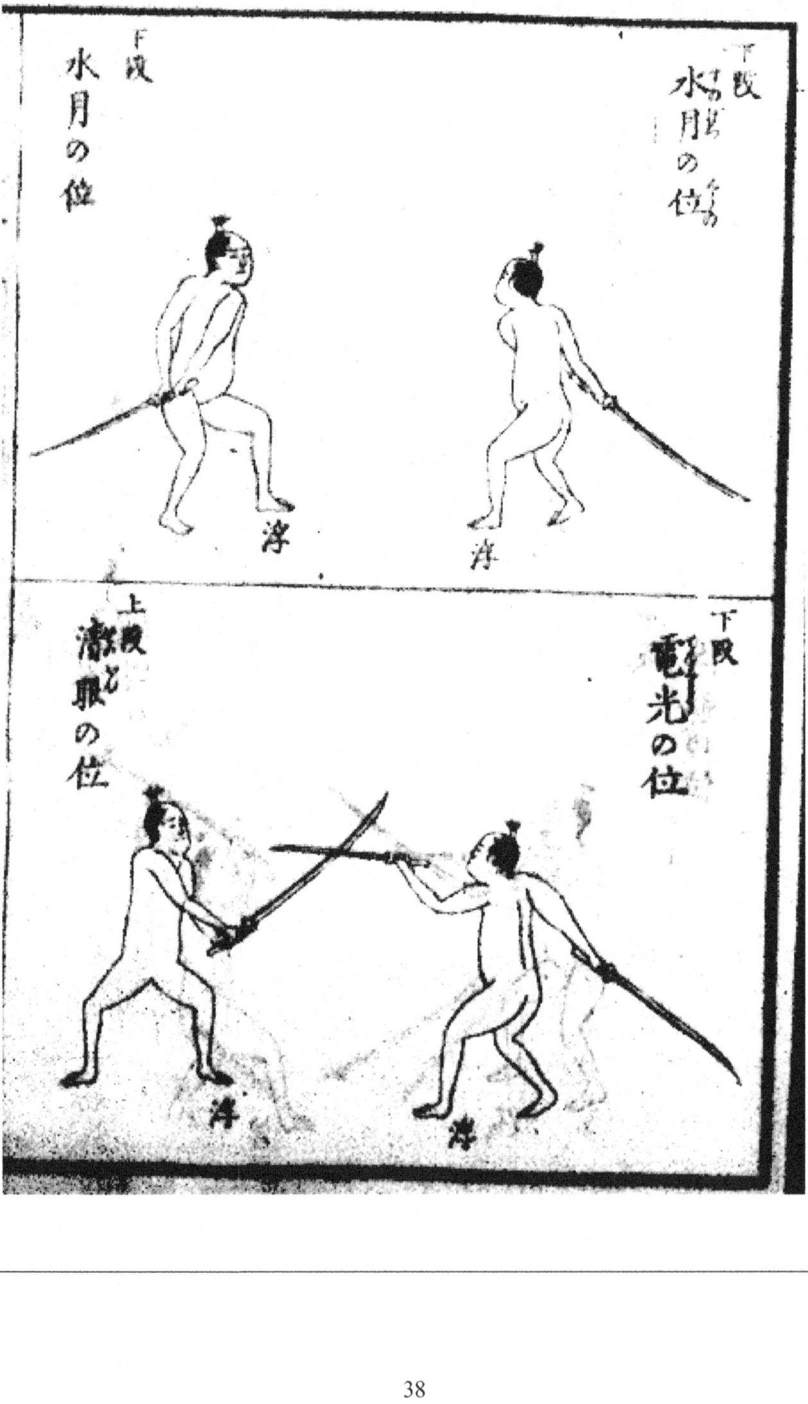

下段
水月の位
下段
水月の位
浮
浮
上段
激眼の位
下段
電光の位
浮
浮

(Left) 下段 水月の位 浮 *Gedan : Suigetsu no Kurai : Uki-Ashi*
Gedan : Moon Reflected on Water Stance: Floating foot

(Right)
下段 水月の位 浮 *Gedan : Suigetsu no Kurai : Uki-Ashi*
Gedan : Moon Reflected on Water Stance : Floating foot

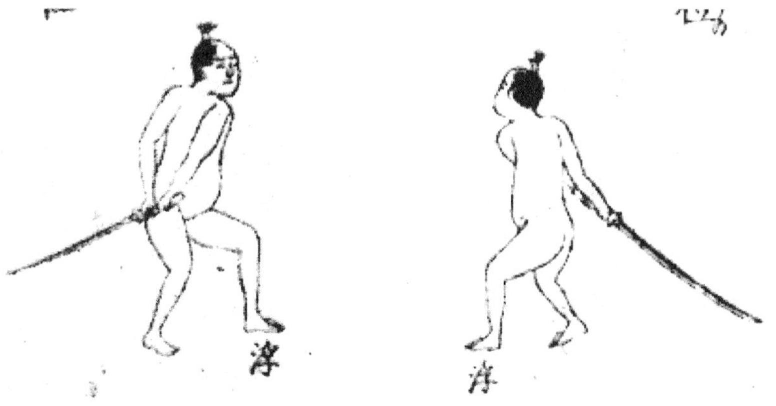

(Left)
下段 電光の位浮 *Gedan : Denko no Kurai : Uki-Ashi*
Gedan : Lightning Stance : Floating foot

(Right)
下段 清眼の位浮 *Gedan : Seigan no Kurai : Uki-Ashi*
Gedan : Clear-eyed : Floating foot

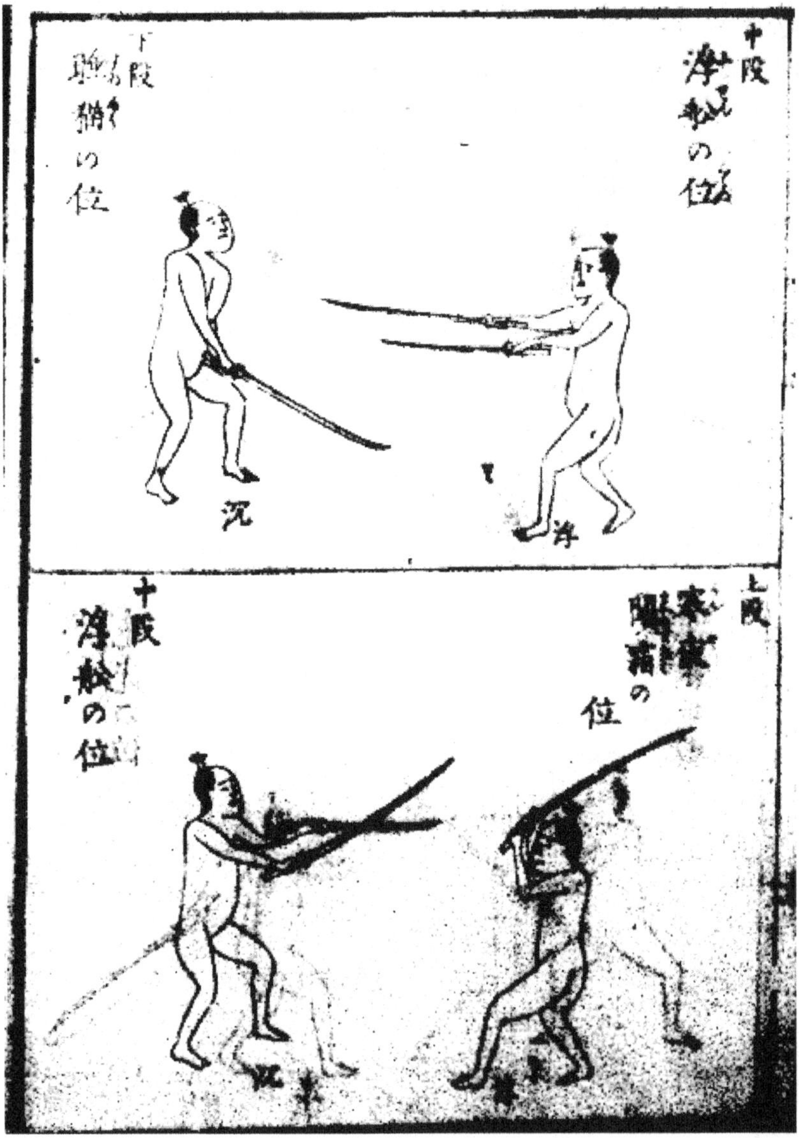
中段
下段
沉
浮
中段
上段

(Left)下段 睡猫 *Gedan : Suibyo no Kurai Shizumu-Ashi*
Gedan : Sleeping Cat Stance : Planted Foot

(Right) 中段浮船の位 *Chudan : Ukibune no Kurai : Uki-Ashi*
Chudan : Floating Boat Stance : Floating Foot

(Left) 中段浮船の位 *Chudan : Ukibune no Kurai : Uki-Ashi*
Chudan : Floating Boat Stance : Floating Foot

(Right) 上段の位
Jodan : Kanyashimo wo Kiku no Kurai : Uki-Ashi
The stance of being able to hear frost crack on a winter's night : Floating Foot

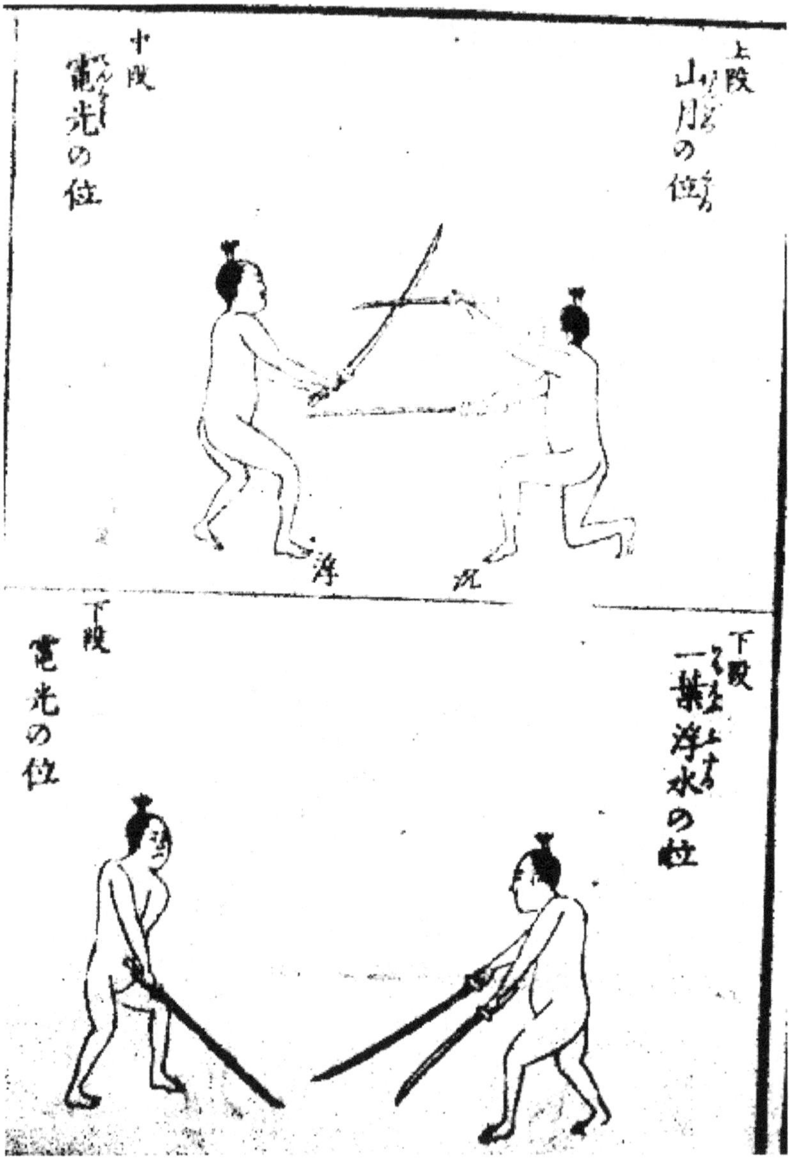
上段
山月の位
中段
電光の位
浮
沈
下段
一葉浮水の位
下段
電光の位

(Left)
中段電光の位浮き *Chudan : Denko no Kurai : Uki-Ashi*
Chudan : Lightning Bolt Stance : Floating Foot

(Right)
上段　山月の位沈 *Jodan : Yamatsuki no Kurai : Shizumu-Ashi*
Jodan : Mountain Moon Stance : Planted Foot.
膝を付ける Plant the knee on the ground.

(Left)下段電光の位 *Gedan : Denko no Kurai : Uki-Ashi*
Gedan : Lightning Bolt Stance : Floating Foot

(Right) 下段一葉浮水の位
Gedan : Ichiefusui no Kurai : Shizumu-Ashi
Gedan: Leaf floating upon water Stance : Planted Foot

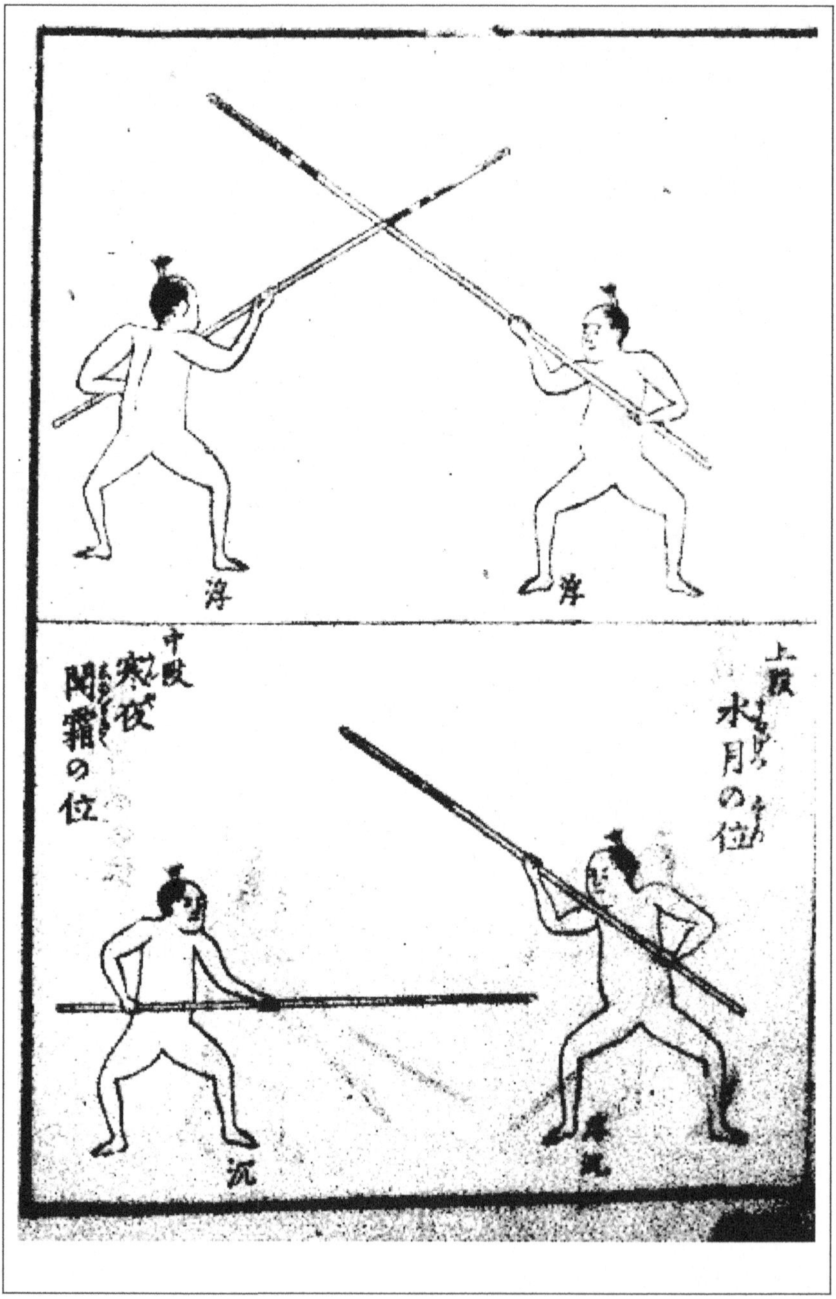
浮
浮
中段
寒夜聞霜の位
上段
水月の位
沉

(Left and right) 浮 Uki- Ashi : Floating foot
Note: The round ball on the end of the spear is padding for training.

(Left)
中段　の位沉
Chudan : Kanyasimowokiku no Kurai : Shizumu-Ashi
Chudan : The stance of being able to hear frost crack on a winter's night : Planted foot

(Right) 上段水月の位　浮沉
Jodan Suigetsu no Kurai Uki-Shizumu Ashi
Jodan : Moon Reflected on Water Stance : Floating/planted foot

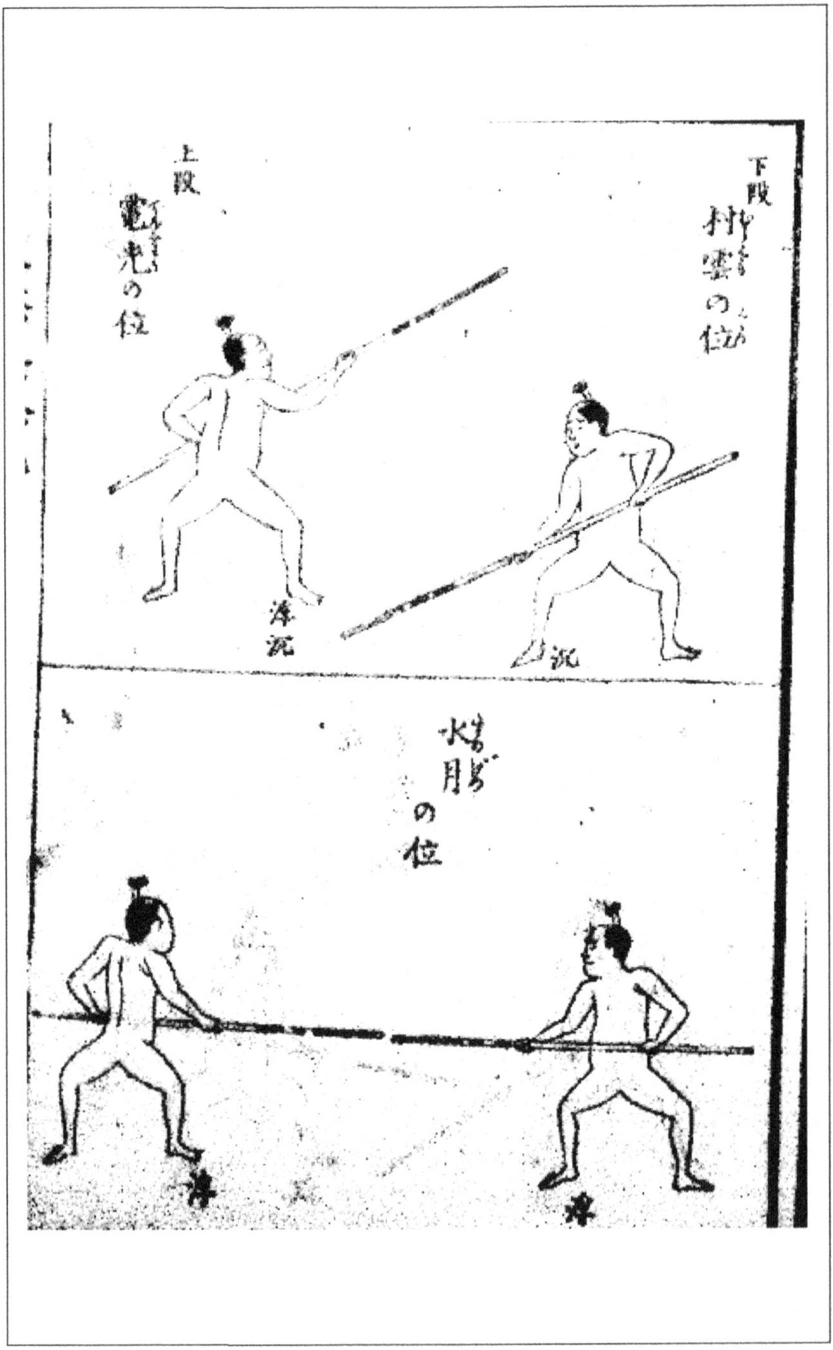
上段
電光の位
下段
村雲の位
浮沈
沈
水月の位
浮
浮

Left)
上段 電光の位下段 浮沈
Jodan: Denko no Kurai : Uki-Shizumu Ashi
Jodan : Lightning Bolt Stance : Floating/Planted foot

(Right)
村雲の位　沈 *Murakumo no Kurai : Shizumu-Ashi*
Cloudy Village : Planted foot

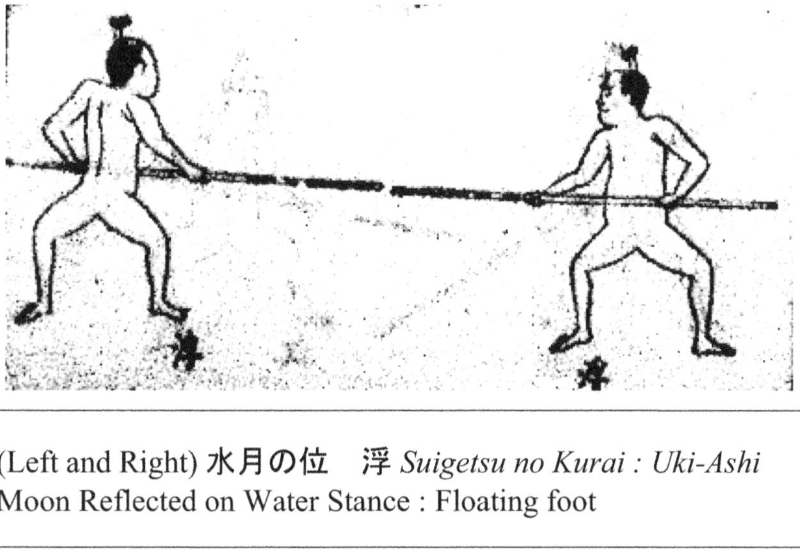

(Left and Right) 水月の位　浮 *Suigetsu no Kurai : Uki-Ashi*
Moon Reflected on Water Stance : Floating foot

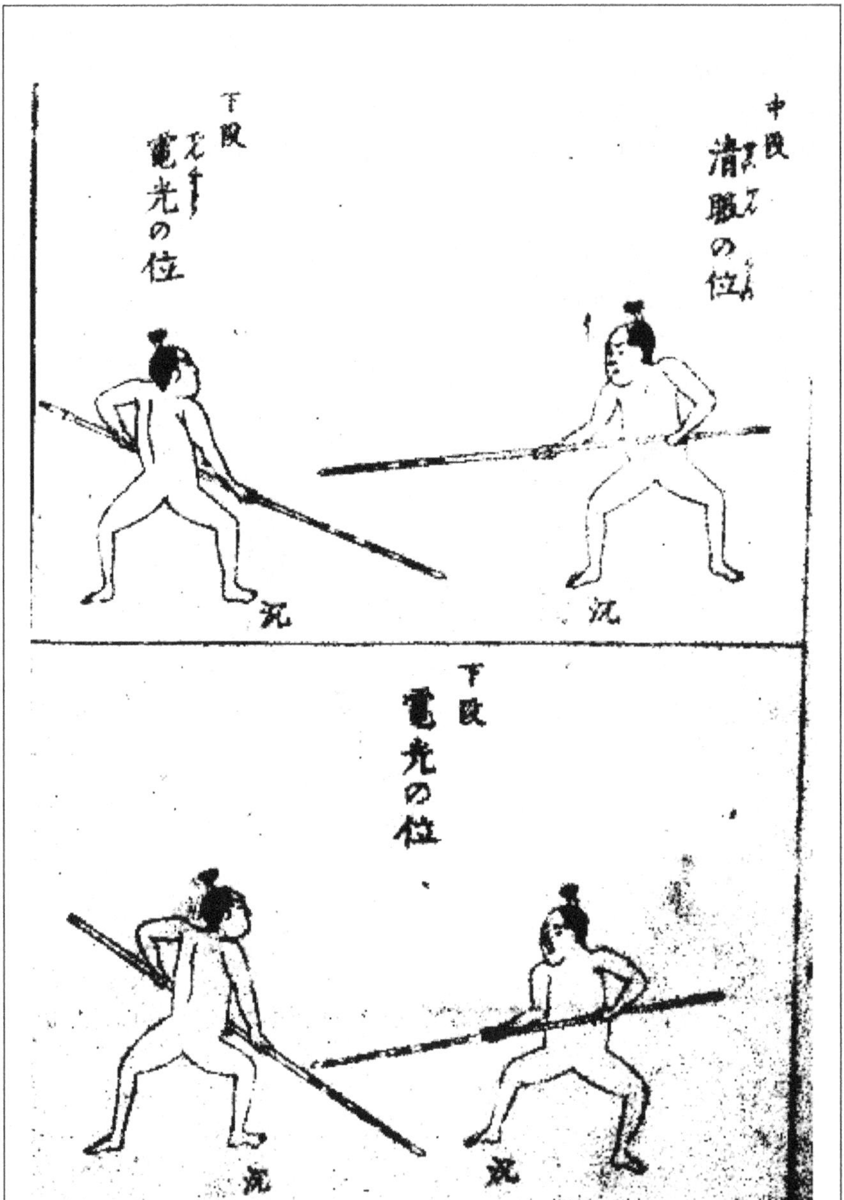
中段
清眼の位
下段
電光の位
下段
電光の位

(Left)
下段電光の位沉 *Gedan : Denko no Kurai : Shizumu-Ashi*
Gedan : Lightning Bolt Stance : Planted foot

(Right)
中段清眼の位沉 *Chudan : Seigan no Kurai : Shizumu-Ashi*
Chudan : Clear-eyed Stance : Planted foot

(Left and Right)下段電光の位沉 Gedan : Denko no Kurai : Shizumu-Ashi
Gedan : Lightning Bolt Stance : Planted foot

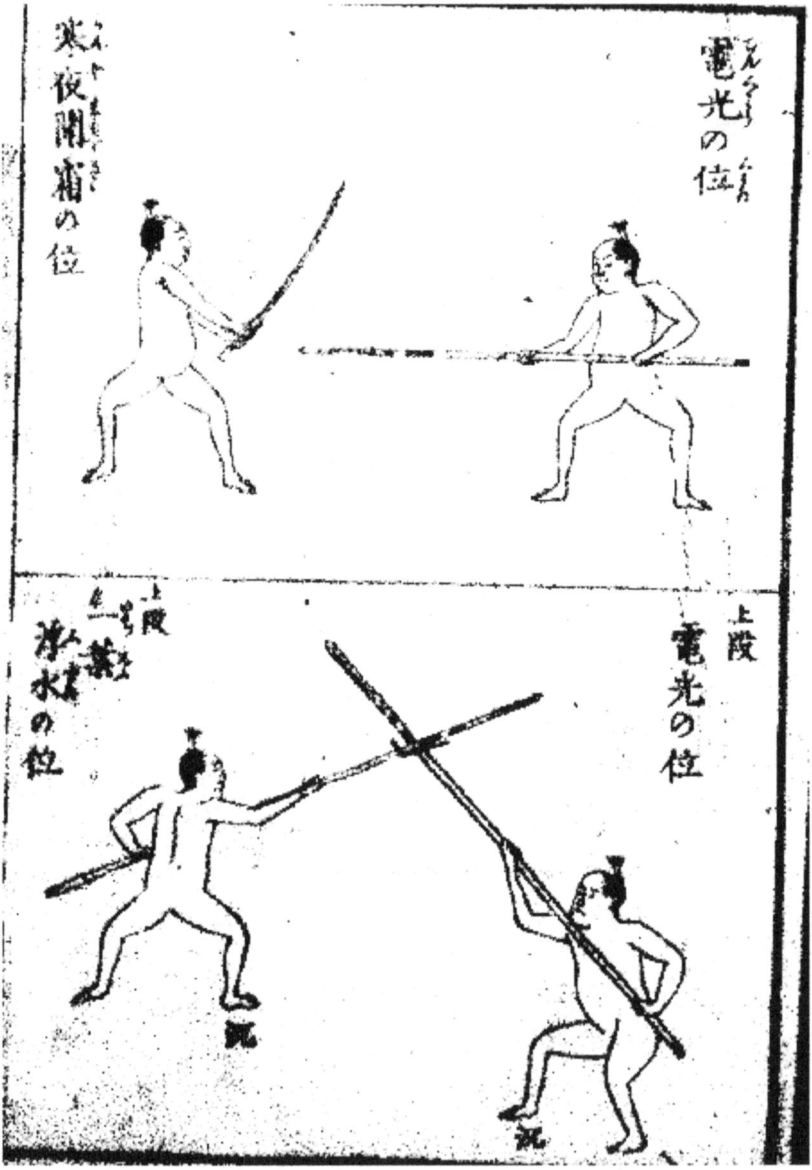
電光の位
寒夜聞霜の位
上段
電光の位
上段
氷水の位

(Left) 上段Error!の位 沈
Kanyashimowokiku no Kurai Shizumu-Ashi
Jodan : The stance of being able to hear frost crack on a winter's night : Planted foot

(Right) 上段電光の位沈 *Jodan: Denko no Kurai Shizumu-Ashi*
Jodan : Lightning Bolt Stance : Planted foot

(Left)
上段　一葉浮水の位沉 Jodan *Ichiefusui no Kurai Shizumu-Ashi*
Jodan : Leaf floating upon water Stance : Planted Foot

(Right)
上段　電光の位沉 *Jodan Denko no Kurai : Shizumu-Ashi*
Jodan : Lightning Bolt Stance : Planted foot.

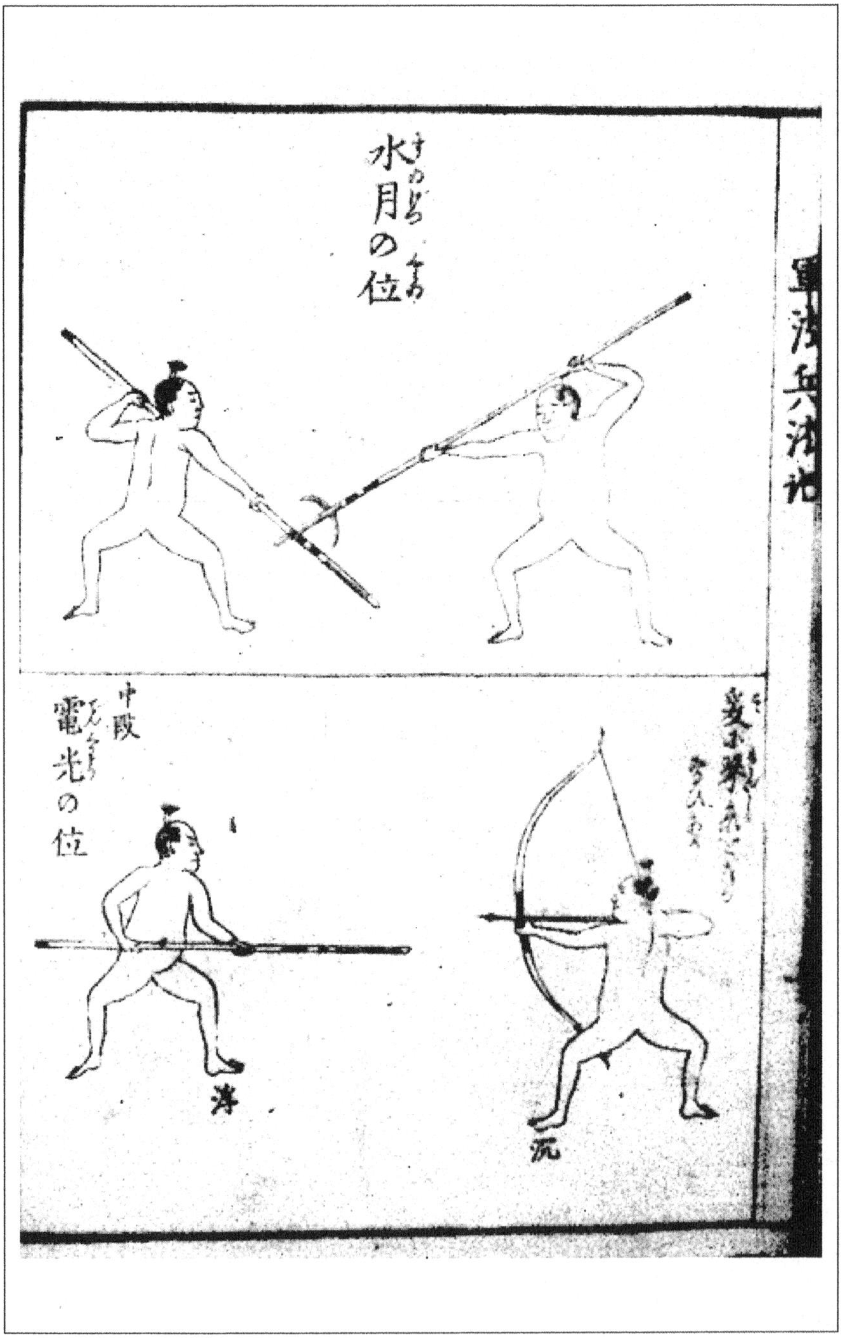
水月の位
中段
電光の位

水月の位 *Suigetsu no Kurai*
Moon Reflected on Water Stance

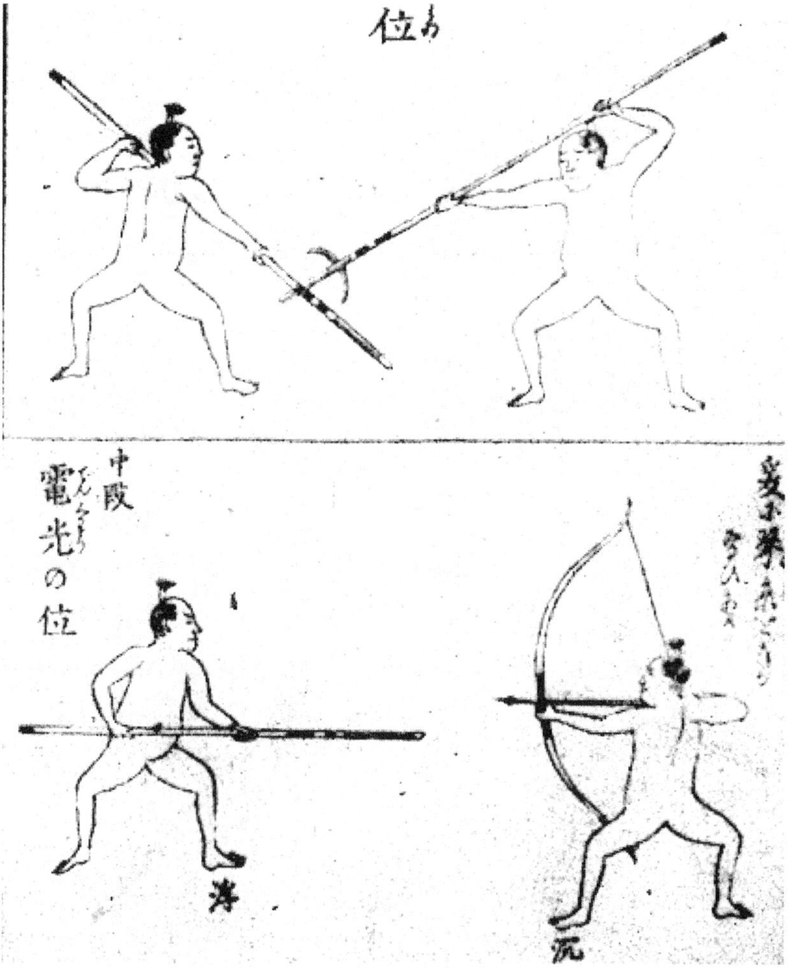

爰琴糸をきる　習ひあり
Here there is a lesson about cutting the cord of the Koto (Japanese guitar)
(Left)
中段電光の位沉　Chudan : Denko no Kurai : Shizumu-Ashi
Chudan : Lightning Bolt Stance : Planted foot

Unarmed Fighting

金鶏獨立 *Kinkei Dokutachi* Golden Bird Standing Alone	懶札衣 *Raisatsui* Languidly Clothed

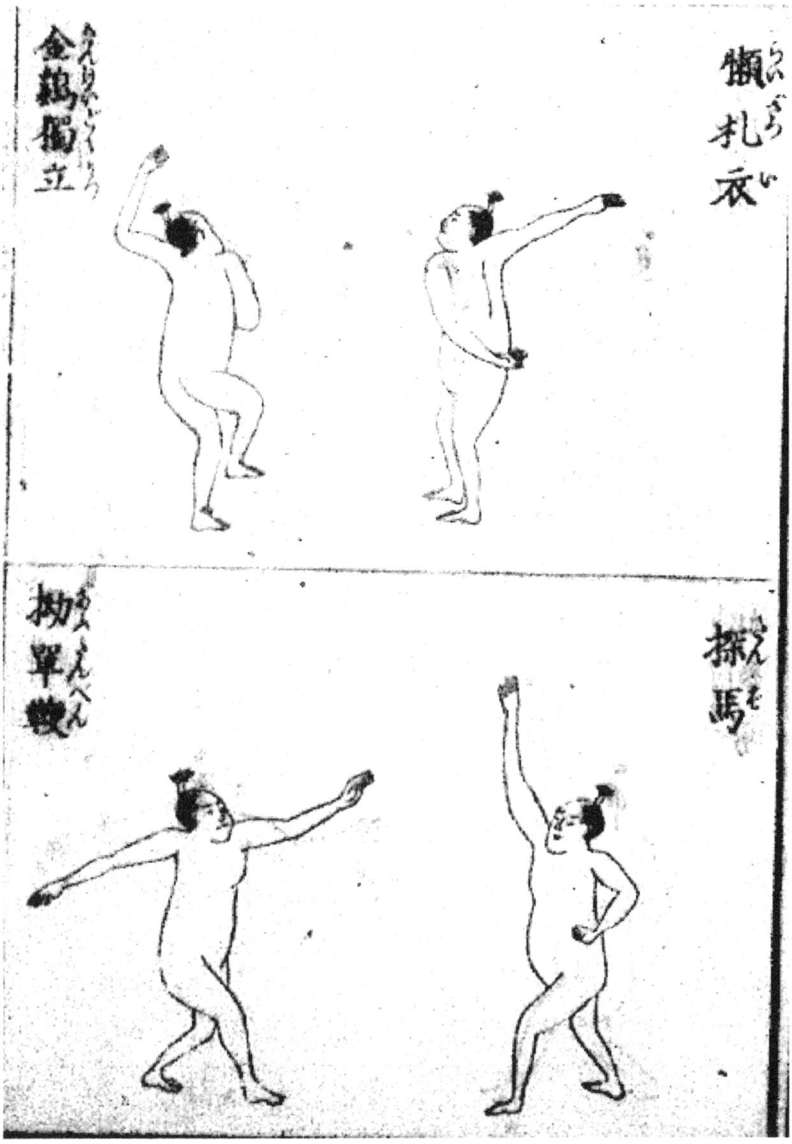

拗單鞭 *Hotanhen* Simple Hurling Change	探馬 *Sonba* Searching Horse

倒騎龍 *Tokiryu* Knight Felling Dragon	七星拳 *Shichiseiken* Seven Star Fist

邱劉勢 *Koryusei* Axe Atop a Hill Stance	縣脚虛 *Kenkyakukyo* Attacking Leg Deceit

埋伏勢 *Maifuku Sei* Buried Flat Kamae	下挿勢 *Chisosei* Lower Penetrating Stance

粘肘勢 *Tenchusei* Twisting Elbow Stance	抛架子 *Hokashi* Hurling Cross

擒拿勢 *Kindasei* Capture and Strike Stance	一霎歩 *Ichishoho* One Step in Light Rain

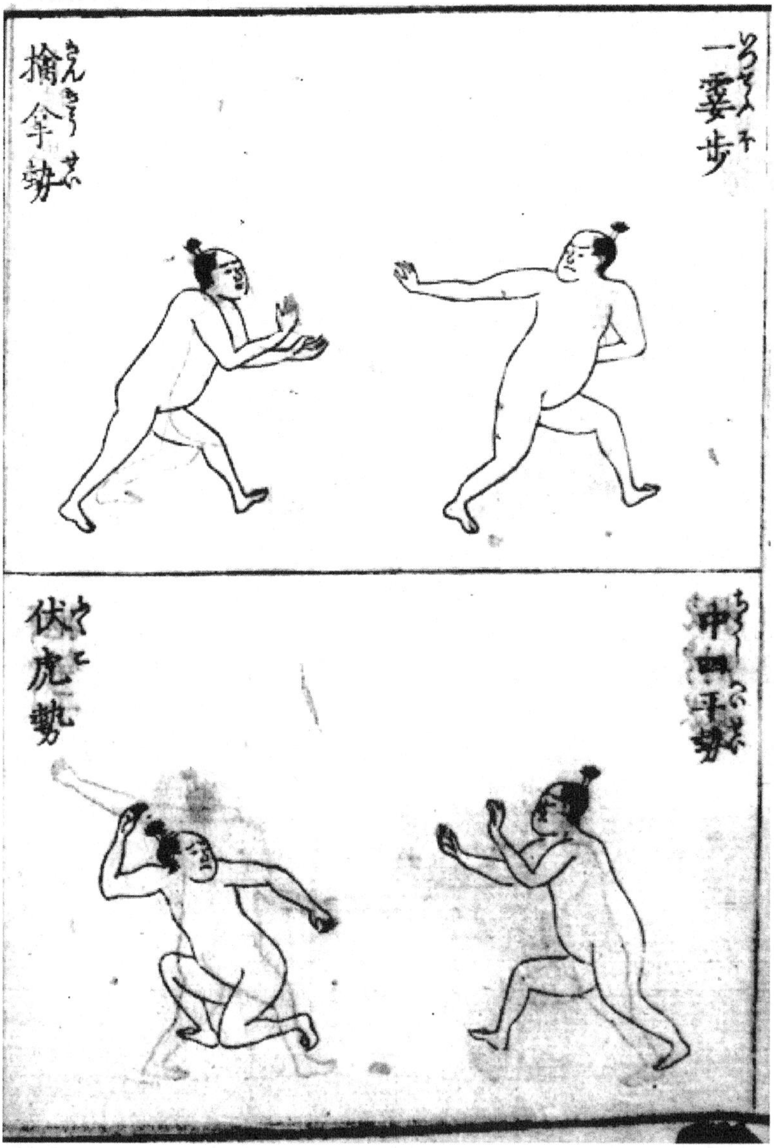

伏虎勢 *Fukkosei* Prone Tiger Stance	中四平勢 *Chushiheisei* Middle Four Directions Stance

倒挿勢 *Tososei* Topple and Push Through Stance	高四平 *Koshitei* Upper Four Directions

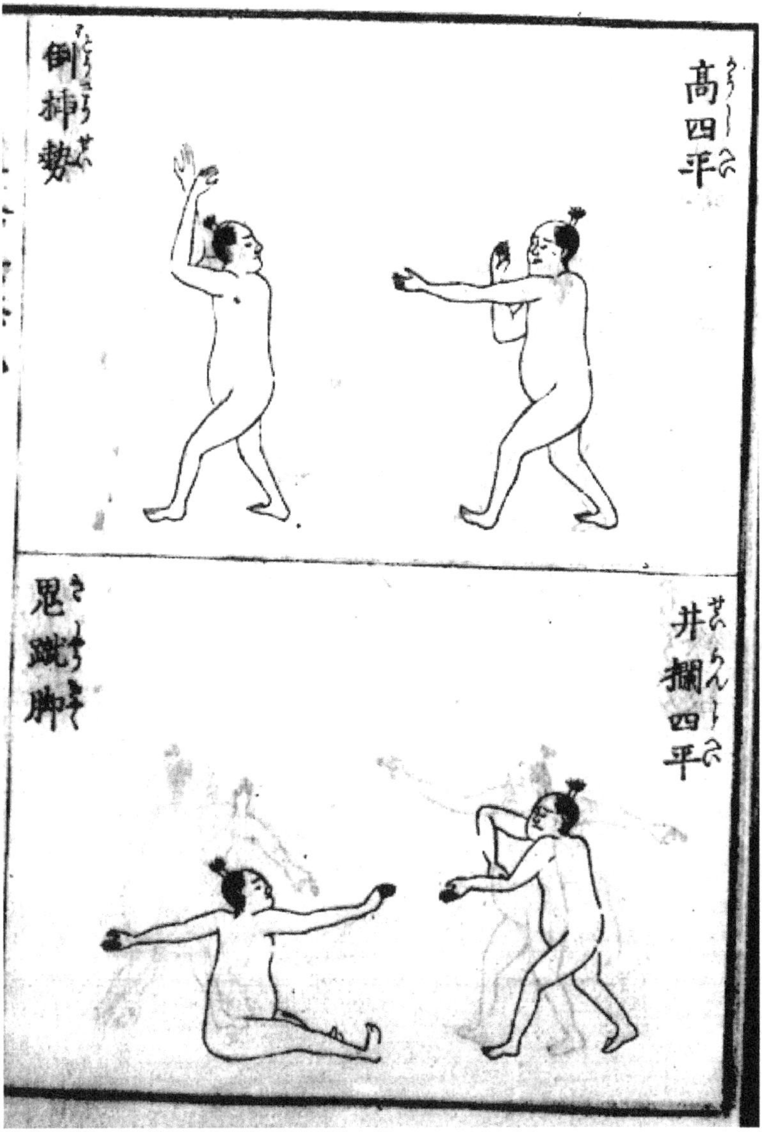

鬼蹴脚 *Kishukyaku* Kicking the Devil's Leg	井欄四平 *Seranshihei* Fence Surrounding a Well

獸頭勢 *Jutosei* Head of a Wild Beast Stance	指當勢 *Shitosei* Striking Finger Stance

一條鞭 *Ichijoben* One Condition Whip	神拳 *Shinken* God Fist

朝陽手 *Choyoshu* Dawn Yang Hand	省地龍 *Shochiryu* Dragon on a Small Piece of Land

騎虎勢 *Kikosei* Tiger Knight Stance	鴈翅 *Ganshi* Wild Goose Feather

當頭砲勢 *Tozusousei* Head High Cannon Stance	拗鸞肘 *Horanchu* Hurling Elbow Akin to the Legendary Chinese Bird

旗鼓勢 *Kitosei* Flag and Drum Stance	順鸞肘 *Junranchu* Elbow of the Mythical Chinese Bird

Translator's Note:

This section of unarmed fighting stances contains only illustrations and the names of the techniques. I realized, however, they are identical to the ones found in a Chinese martial arts compendium called *Treatise on Armament Technology*. This massive 240 volume work was compiled in 1621 by Mao Yuanyi 茅元儀 (1594–1640) is known as the Bubishi. Upon further research I located a book called *Secrets of the Sword and Spear* 剣鎗秘術討清剣舞学・棒拳秘術討清舞学 by Ishibashi Nakawa. The book, published in the 28th year of Meiji 1895, transcribes the meanings of 9 of the stances from Chinese into Japanese. It is not clear why he only selected 9 out of the 32 techniques shown in the *Treatise on Armament Technology* as well as *A Quick Guide to Martial Arts.*

Treatise on Armament Technology 1621	*Secrets of the Sword and Spear 1895*

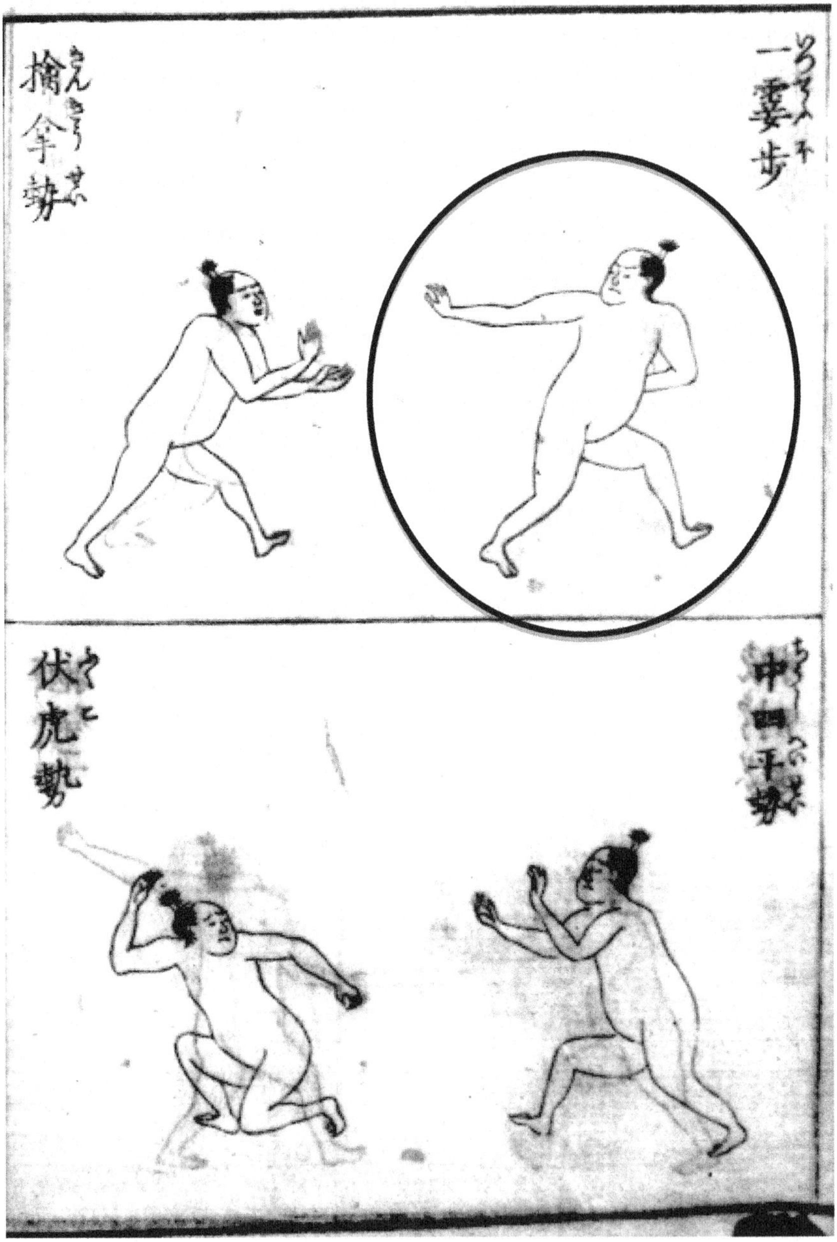
一霎歩
擒拿勢
中四平勢
伏虎勢

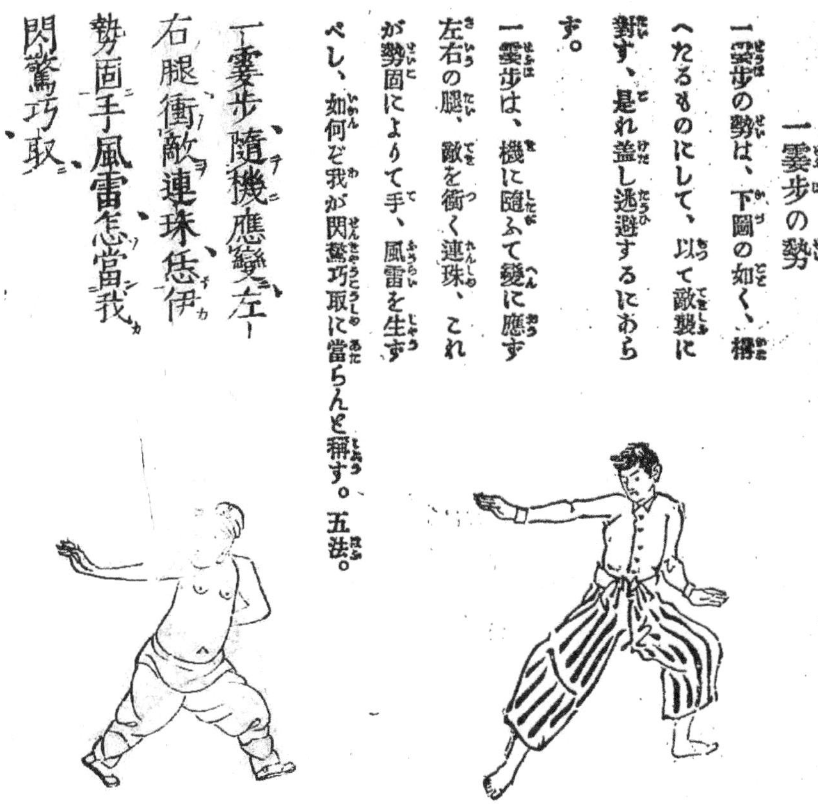
一霎歩の勢
一霎歩の勢は、下圖の如く、構へたるものにして、以て敵襲に對す、是れ蓋し逃避するにあらず。
一霎歩は、機に隨ふて變に應ず左右の腿、敵を衝く連珠、これが勢固によりて手、風雷を生ずべし、如何ぞ我が閃驚巧取に當らんと稱す。五法。
一霎歩隨機應變、左右腿衝敵連珠、恁伊勢固手風雷、怎當我閃驚巧取、

Ichishoho
One Step in Light Rain

For the stance called One Step in Light Rain the body should be positioned as is shown in the illustration below. It is generally showing evasion in the face of the enemy's attack.

The meaning of One Step in Light Rain is to deftly shift your position at the right moment. The opponent kicks out with the left and right legs in rapid succession. When his movement stops your fist should fly out like wind and thunder. The movement should be as surprising as a flash of lightning followed by a skilled attack.

高四平
倒挿勢
井欄四平
鬼蹴脚

井欄四平の勢

井欄四平の勢は、下圖の如く、構へたるものにして、以て敵手の施爲に對するに在り。井欄四平の勢、直ちに進んで臁を剪て、膝を踢り頭に當たる、滾穿劈靠、一鈎を抹す、蓋し鐵樣の將軍も亦た走ると稱す。七法。

井欄四平直進、剪臁、踢膝當頭滾穿劈靠、抹一鈎、鐵樣將軍也走、

Seranshihei
Fence Surrounding a Well

For the stance known as Fence Surrounding a Well the body should be positioned as sown in the illustration below. This Kamae, or stance, in in response to the enemy's intent. With Fence Surrounding a Well you move directly in with a slicing attack to the midsection. Kick out at the knees and head-butt. You completely obliterate the opponent with rolling strikes, straight strikes, breaking strikes or a single hard shove.

It is also referred to as the method that will allow you to cause even an iron Shogun to run.

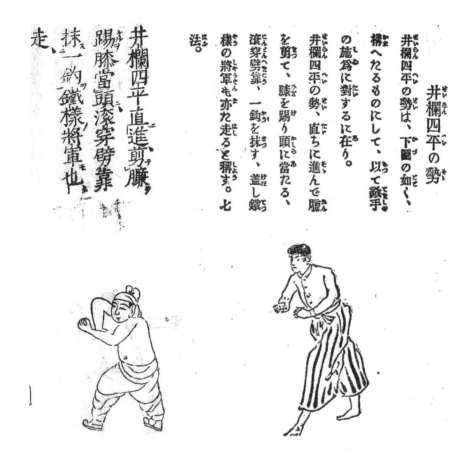

指當勢
獸頭勢
神拳
一條鞭

指當の勢

指當の勢は、下圖の如く、構へたるものにして、以て敵手の來搏に對するに在り。

指南の勢は、是れ箇の丁法とす他進み難く、我れ好く向ふ、前踢膝滾して、餘亦た上面に及ぶ急に回歩して短紅拳を顚すと稱す。九法。

指當勢、是箇丁法、他難進、我好向、前踢膝滚躦上面、急回歩顚短紅拳、

Shitonosei
Attacking With the Fingers

The body positioning for Attacking With the Fingers is as shown in the illustration below. You are ready to responds to the opponent's attempt to seize you.

A detail on the body positioning of this Kamae passed down by instructors is that it is a Choho or stance that resembles the Kanji 丁. It is hard for the hated enemy to advance but it is easy for you to move in on him. With the front leg, kick over his knee. From there strike to the upper part of the face. Another way of thinking of it is to quickly step around and knock the opponent down with a "short red punch."

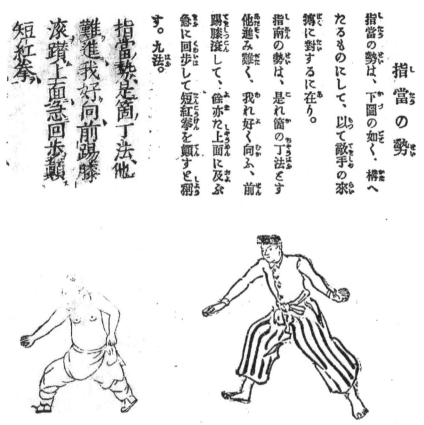

指當勢
獸頭勢
神拳
一條鞭

獸頭の勢

獸頭の勢は、下圖の如く、構へたるものにして、以て指當に對す。
指當、獸頭互角の勢、何れか優何れか劣たるを知らす。
獸頭の勢、牌の如くにして、挨進し而して快脚我に遇ふて慌忙低驚し、高く取て他防ぎ難し、接短して紅を披き上を衝くと稱す。十法。

獸頭勢、如牌挨進恁
快脚遇我慌忙低驚
高取他難防接短披
紅衝上。

Jutosei
Wild Beast Head Stance

The proper stance for Wild Beast Head Stance is as shown in the illustration below. It stands in contrast to the previous technique, Attacking With the Fingers. You should understand that both Attacking With the Fingers and Wild Beast Head Stance are equivalent. Know that both are highly refined yet neither is inferior to the other.

The feeling of Wild Beast Head Stance is charging forward like you are attacking with a shield. Upon facing the rapid charge of your feet, the enemy becomes disorganized. If you startle him low then attack high it will prove hard for the hated enemy to guard.

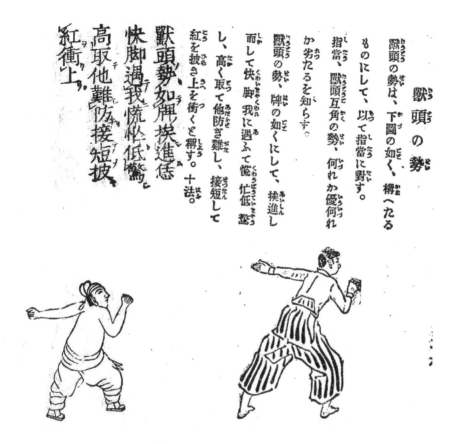

Another way to look at it is you should knock away his close in short attacks and strike in from above.

中四平の勢

中四平の勢は、下圖の如く構へたるものにして、以て敵手の下搏に對す。

中四平の勢は、實に固を推す、硬く攻進す、快腿來り難し、雙手して他の單手に逼る、短打して以て熟するを乖と爲すと稱す。十一法。

中四平勢實推固硬
攻進快腿難來雙手
逼他單手短打以熟
爲乖

Chushiheisei
Middle Four Directions Stance

The way you should go into Middle Four Directions Stance as is shown in the illustration below. This is used in response to low attacks by the opponent's fists. You should think of Middle Four Directions Stance as being really hard. You are attacking strongly, making it hard for an opponent with fast footwork to enter. Use both hands when attacking to overwhelm the hated enemy's one hand.

It is best to consider this technique as being best suited for a person who has trained short strikes extensively.

一霎步
擒拿勢
中四平勢
伏虎勢

伏虎の勢

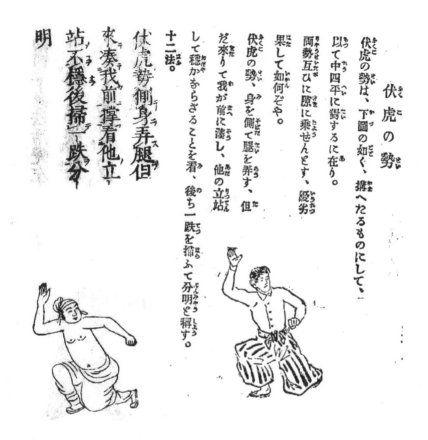

伏虎の勢は、下圖の如く、搆へたるものにして、一以て中四平に對するに在り。兩勢互ひに隙に乘せんとす、優劣果して如何ぞや。

伏虎の勢、身を側て腿を弄す、但だ來りて我が前に湊し、他の立站して穩かならざることを看、後ち一跌を掃ふて分明と稱す。十二法。

伏虎勢側身弄腿但來湊我前撑看他立站不穩後掃一跌分明

Fukkosei
Prone Tiger Stance

The Body positioning of Prone Tiger Stance is as shown in the illustration below. It should be viewed in opposition or contrast to Middle Four Direction Stance. Neither of these stances allow an appropriate opening for the opponent to slip by. It is all but impossible to discern which stance is better than the other.

The feeling of Prone Tiger Stance is having the body sideways with the leg out taunting and inviting. When the enemy comes in, your body weight should shift onto the forward leg. The focus of this stance is the seeing the hated enemy's balance point become lost, in one clear mouton sweep his leg away causing him to stumble.

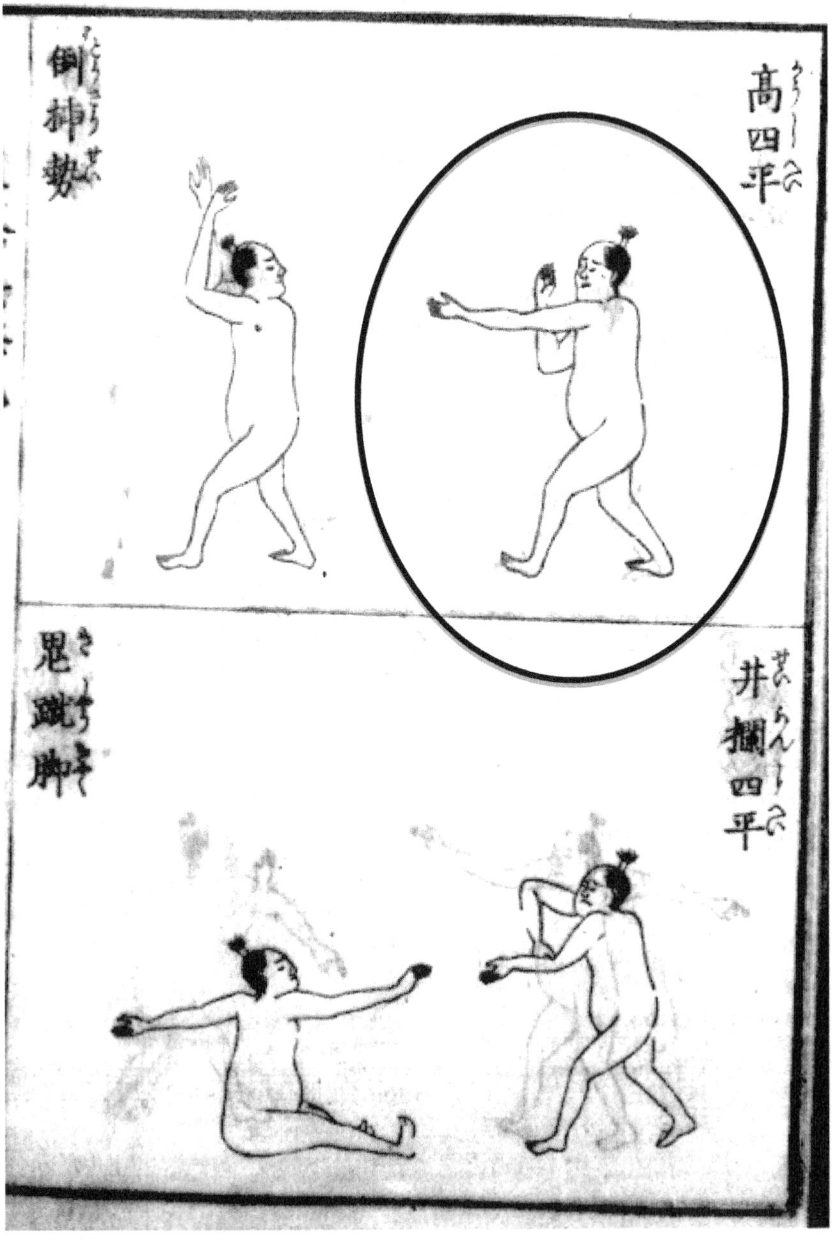

高四平
倒插勢
井攔四平
鬼蹴脚

高四平の勢

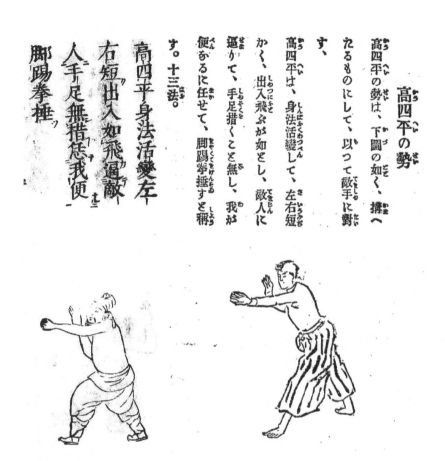

高四平の勢は、下圖の如く、搆へたるものにして、以つて敵手に對す、

高四平は、身法活變して、左右短かく、出入飛ぶが如とし、敵人に逼りて、手足措くこと無し、我が便あるに任せて、脚踢拳捶すと稱す。十三法。

高四平身法活變左右短出入如飛逼敵人手足無措恁我便脚踢拳捶

Koshitei

Upper Four Directions

The stance for Upper Four Directions is as shown in the below illustration. You should face off against the opponent like this. The meaning of Upper Four Directions is allowing the body to move freely and adapt to any situation. It uses short movements to the left and right as you fly in and out. The enemy approaches but he is unable to lay his hands on you.

The focus of this technique is entirely up to you. Kick out with your leg or lash out with your fists as suits you.

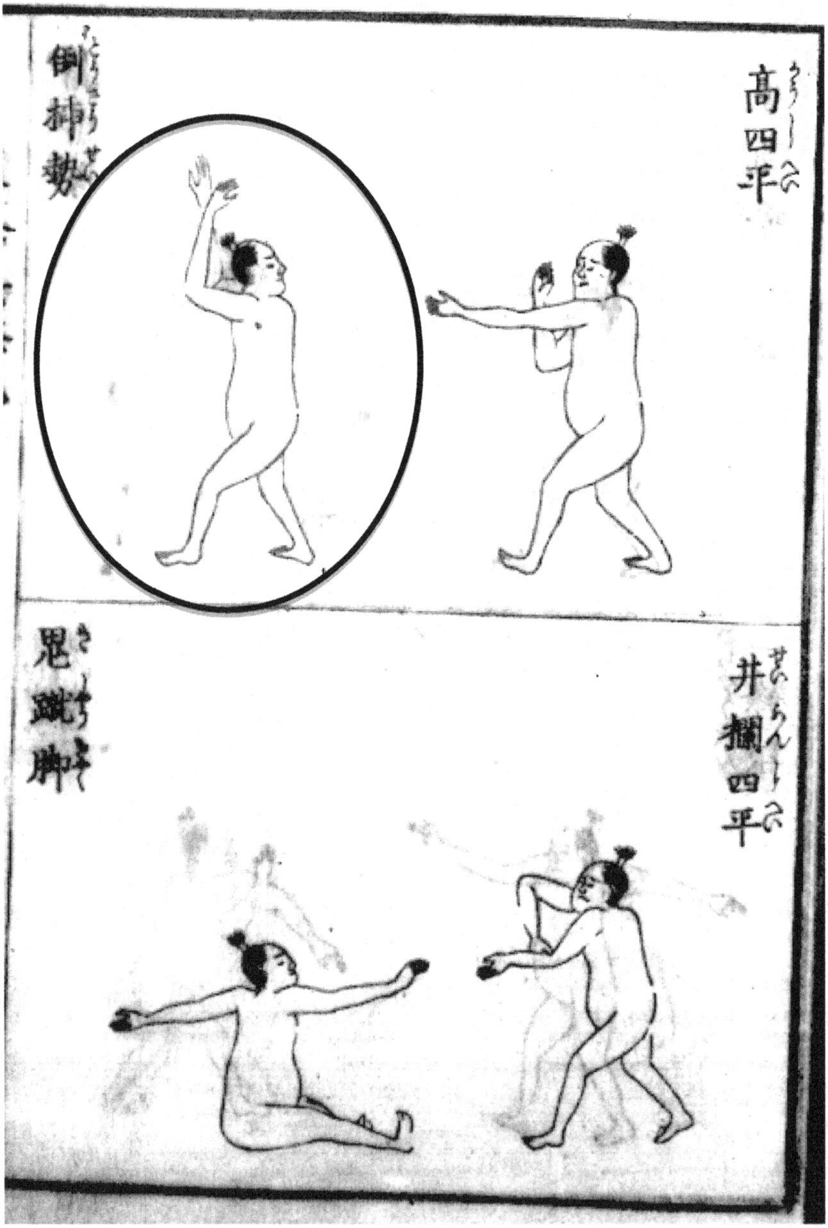
高四平
倒挿勢
井欄四平
鬼蹴脚

倒挿の勢

倒挿の勢は、下図の如く、挿へたるものにして、以て高四平に對す。

高四平は剛、倒挿は優、勝敗如何未だ知るべからず。

倒挿の勢、與に招架せず、腿に靠りて快く他を討ず、是れ贏つとす、背弓歩を進めて、遅停すること莫く、打つこと谷聲の相應するが如しと稱す。十四法

倒挿勢不與招架靠
腿快討他之贏背弓
進歩莫遅停打如谷
聲相應

Tososei
Topple and Push Through Stance

The stance known as Topple and Push Through Stance is done as shown in the illustration below. It is in contrast to Upper Four Directions.

As to how a direct contest between Upper Four Directions, which is strong like iron, or Topple and Push Through Stance, which is refined, the only thing that can be understood is that it cannot be decided.

When in Topple and Push Through Stance you do not resist the opponent's attacks. You rely on your legs and dart strikes at the enemy. The way you achieve victory is to step behind him, without slowing or stopping. The feeling of this Kamae is striking like the echo reverberating back off a valley.

一霎步
擒拿勢
中四平勢
伏虎勢

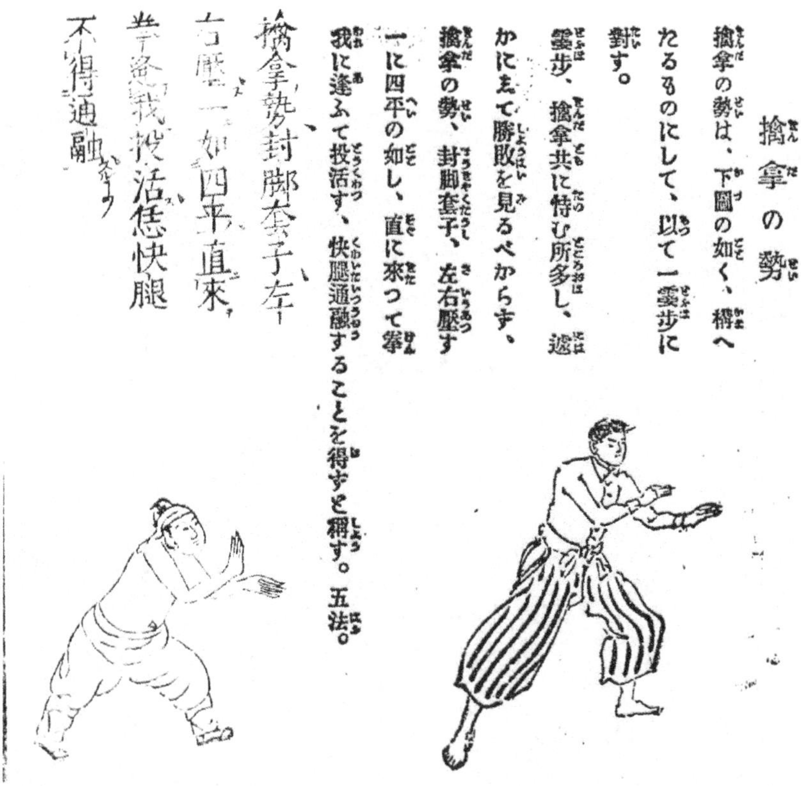

擒拿の勢

擒拿の勢は、下圖の如く、構へたるものにして、以て一霎歩に對す。

霎歩、擒拿共に恃む所多し、遽かにまて勝敗を見るべからず、擒拿の勢、封脚套子、左右壓す一に四平の如し、直に來つて拳我に逢ふて投活す、快腿通融することを得ずと稱す。五法。

擒拿勢封脚套子左右壓一如四平直來拳逢我投活恁快腿不得通融

擒拿勢 *Kindasei*
Capture and Strike Stance

For Capture and Strike Stance the body should be positioned as is shown in the illustration below. It stands in contrast to One Step in Light Rain.

Both I One Step in Light Rain and Capture and Strike Stance have a lot of elements that parallel each other and have to be considered simultaneously. That being said you should not try to focus on any one element to grant you success.

The feeling of Capture and Strike Stance should be about stopping the opponent's movement with your swift footwork. Your left and right pressure makes it seem as if you are in four places at the same time. Should a straight punch come in you would completely tear it apart. It is referred to as the technique that stops the smooth fast flow of the opponent.

Staff Fighting

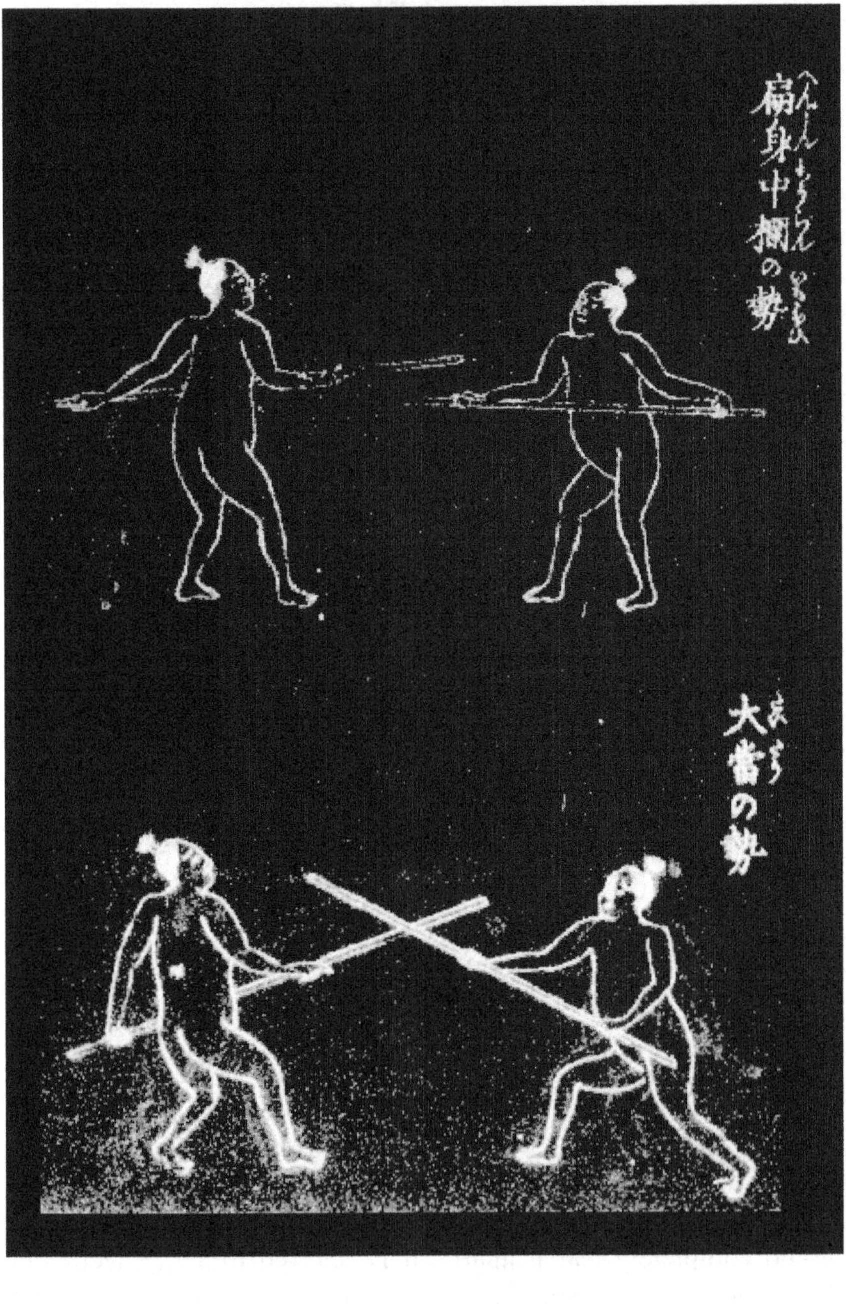

扁身中欄の勢 *Henshinchuran no Ikioi*

Level Body Mid-Field Stance

大當の勢 *Taito no Ikioi*

Big Strike Stance

大剪の勢 *Taizen no Ikioi*

Great Cut Stance

僊人棒盤の勢 *Senninhohan no Ikioi*

Mountain Ascetic Bo Slab Stance

大吊の勢 *Tairyo no Ikioi*
Big Hanging Stance

齊眉殺の勢　*Seihisatsu no Ikioi*
Killing Strike to the Eyebrow Stance

倒頭の勢 *Toto no Ikioi*
Toppling the Head Stance

下穿の勢 *Kasen no Ikioi*
Lower Strike Stance

閃腰剪の勢　*Senyosen no Ikioi*
Lightning Slice to the Waist Stance

下接の勢　*Kasefu no Ikioi*
Lower Strike Stance

滴水の勢 *Tekisui no Ikioi*

Water Droplet Stance

直符送書の勢 *Chokufusosho no Ikioi*

Straight Talisman Sent Letter Stance

走馬回頭の勢 *Sobakaito no Ikioi*
Running Horse Spinning Head Stance

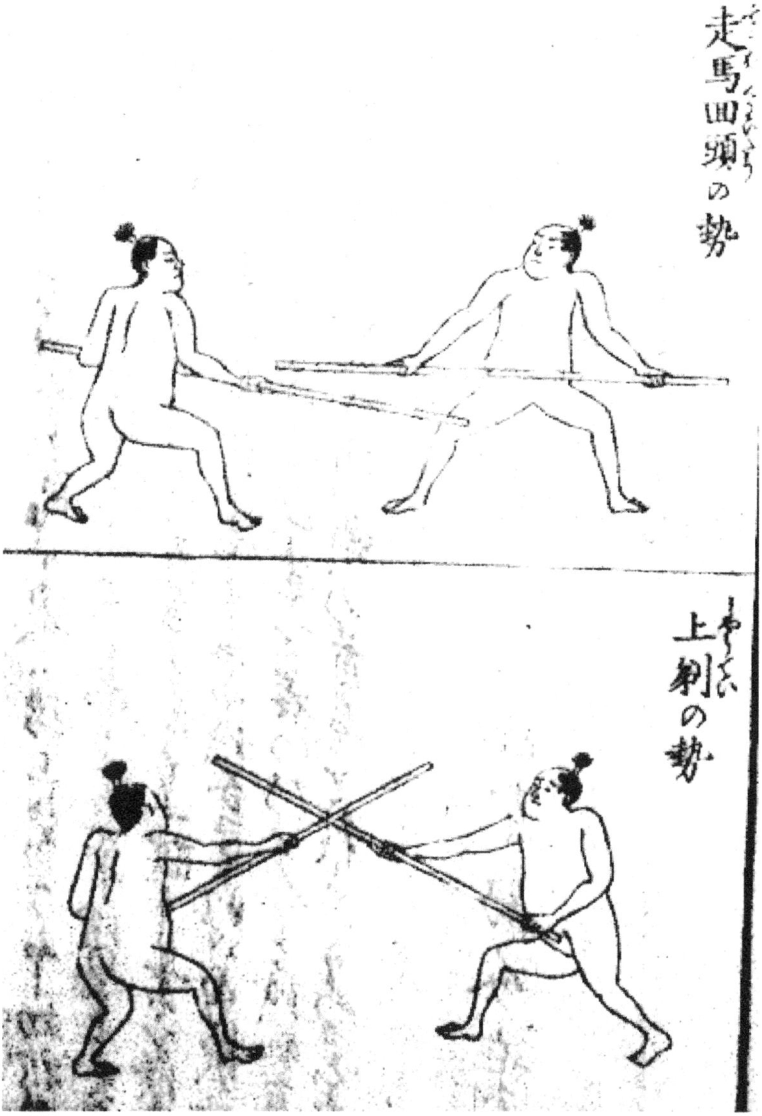

上剃の勢　*Jotei no Ikioi*
Upper Shave Stance

Translator's Note :

As with the previous Unarmed Fighting stances, the Staff Fighting stances all appear in *Treatise on Armament Technology* published in 1621. The following section presents the relevant pages from *Treatise on Armament Technology* on top and the corresponding illustrations from *A Quick Guide to Martial Arts* below.

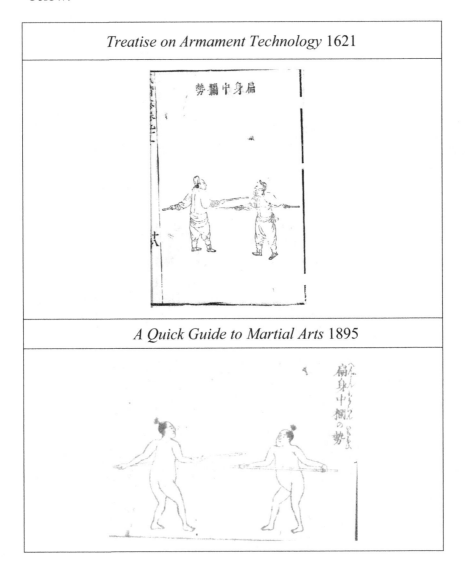

Treatise on Armament Technology 1621

A Quick Guide to Martial Arts 1895

扁身中攔勢

扁身中攔の勢

大當勢

大當の勢

大勇勢

仙人捧盤勢

大字勢

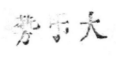

齊眉殺勢

倒頭勢

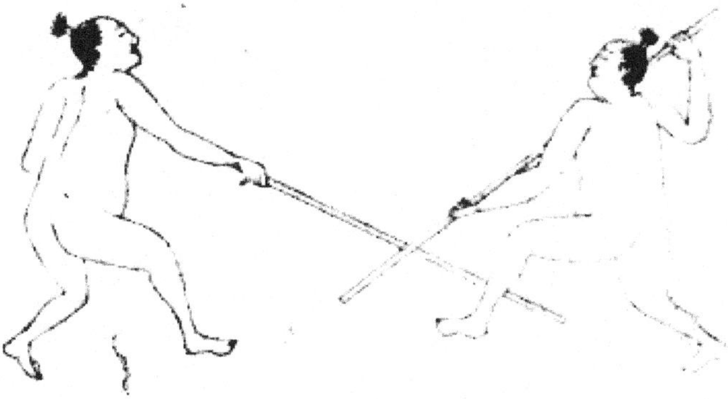

下穿勢

閃腰剪勢

の勢

勢接下

滴水勢

直符送書勢

走馬回頭勢

上剃勢

Strategies and the Inner Secrets Scroll

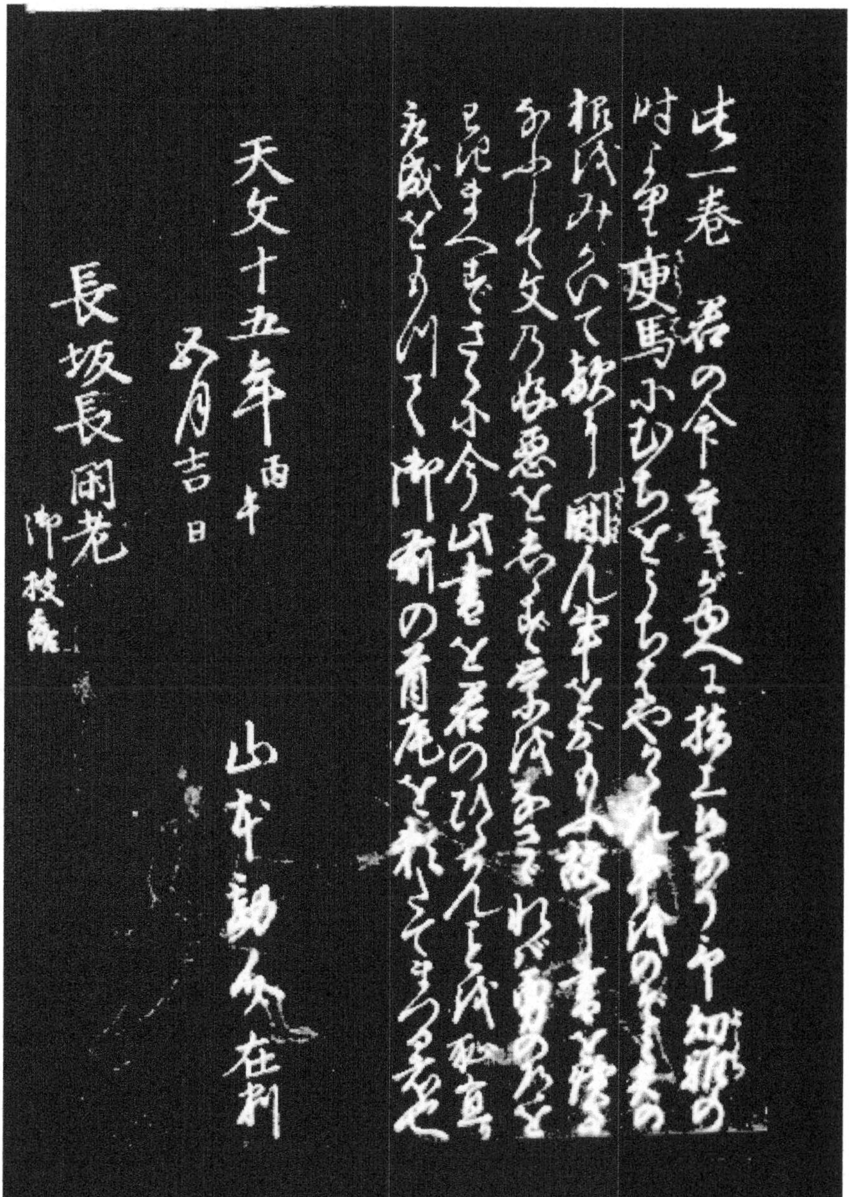

天文十五年丙午
五月吉日
山本勘介 在判
長坂長閑老
御披露

As the life of your lord is of the upmost importance, I have crafted this scroll. From a young age I recall being enthralled with horse-riding and often thought of fighting enemies while polishing the shafts of arrows. For this reason when reading a document I do not dwell on whether or not the writing is good or lacking but if it instills a sense of bravery in me. Further, you should endeavor to become the kind of subject that uses such knowledge to serve your lord without shame and to complete all tasks assigned to you successfully and without fail.

Fifteenth year of Tenbun May First 1546
Yamamoto Dokisai (Dokisai is his Buddhist name)
Kansuke
Haruyuki

Introduction by the revered elder
Nagasaka Chokan (?－1582)

▲入身の事

世にの入身といふハ身をすてゝ捕とも又ハ十文字に捕るなりて
また其の手をもちてへ入所より今ゐる所にあらずしもそのハ敵の
切手へ出る所より門をいふ是にニッの法あり敵を捕の法
それは表方と裏とありて何れにもなかれ中段に出て入てつかんとする
所にあるにおふかたより捕とすれハ遠近の法ありとも よくのべし
是も其外に敵をつかまへの所にある

▲追かけ者仕様の事

追かけ者ハ二ッの所有 是追掛の時ハ浮の勢ひをもちて
所の後とてもちらざるべしかふなどちらくみてもちうちまつて
又たちかへる時ハ逃ても勢ひをぬからざるべし其ときは追の事を

の事
Nyushin no Koto
Entering With Your Body

Generally the meaning of the term Nyushin 入身 is to stop the movement of the Yari with the Tachi. You can also use a Juji-Kagi Yari, or a hooked cross shaped headed spear, to catch the opponent's spear and enter Temoto 手元, where the opponent's hands hold the spear. What is written here is a method for breaking the opponent's Kamae, or stance.

There are three ways of thinking for those entering the gate, which is another way of saying entering deep into the enemy's space. If you detect the Kehai 気配, or the intention, of the opponent you should take Daijodan no Kamae. Should you detect the enemy's Keihai coming from the right, you should go into Chudan Kamae while visualizing doing a Tsuki 突, or straight thrust. When you sense Keihai in front of you enter while staying aware the space near you and farther away as well. This is the best method for detecting the Keihai of the enemy.

める事
Oikake Mono no Shitomere Koto
How to Strike Down an Escaping Samurai

With regards to pursuing a fleeing soldier there are two things taught. When striking while pursuing you should make use of techniques that have Uki-ashi and strike with a sweeping Gedan cut to the lower part of the body. You should take care with your distancing as though it seems you are close enough, you may end up missing your target entirely.

Should the enemy come about you should, initially, drop back a step thereby lessoning the opponent's energy. Here you are required to evaluate the relative distance near or far to the opponent.

There is a Kuden.

▲居合(いあひ)の事

凡剣術にハ二ツの品あり さやより抜はなして打を曲(きよく)として稽古する

時ハ諸芸の術の外にあるこれを名て居合といふなり 居合ハ

みえぬ又あり其上にも太刀まで抜はなす取手に此度を

その術をも学てのち居合をは二の事にあり 剣術を常とする者

これはちらくり太刀の事なれば学ぶべし 鍛錬(たんれん)剣術を常とする者はすべく

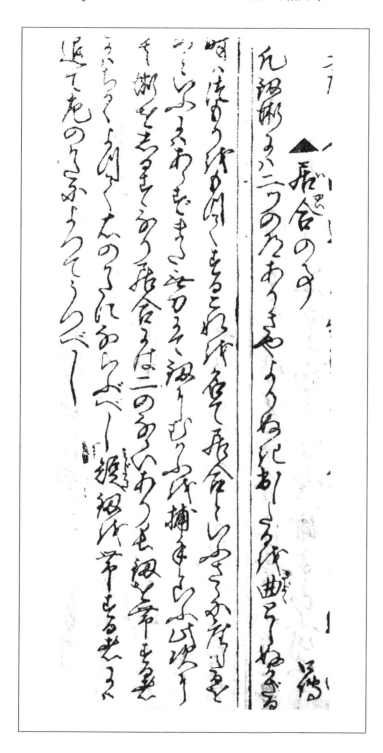

返て後の事ふかくするようにすべし

の事
Iai no Koto
Sword Drawing

This section will have to be balanced with what was written in the previous chapters. This is the thing that has been given the name Iai. However, Iai is not done exclusively from a seated position. It can also refer to when you take down an opponent armed with a sword when you are Muto, or without a sword. Next that technique will be explained.

There are two techniques in Iai. For opponents with a long sword in their belt, close in until you are aligned with their right shoulder. For opponents with a short sword, you should drop back and cut in toward the opponent's right shoulder.

▲捕手のこと

捕手は長短によりて細作多くあるなり すなはちちくよりて細とうご
つまて老人をばいつはりてせんとするもの三ツの要あるべし 又たく
残賊をもつて細の諸篇いふまでもなく四肢の要を心得て残を縦
封じて是をもつてのかれひとつ絶ゆるもひとつの心
得たりとも是と常あるもののはおそれともいかほどすぐれたる者も
あるはいつもべしするとの者をばかるの事へ入り歩行さきとも
かつ抑捕手は合せふしとするもののぐらふ合せめしにぞなる

の事

Torite no Koto

Unarmed Fighting

Torite refers to when you are fighting without any sort of blade, long or short and you are against a person swinging a sword. You deceive this person and take the advantage with your Ashi Sabaki, or footwork, along with three main points. These will be briefly detailed below. Abbreviated below.

On the battlefield, when the swords do not end the fight, battling on with feet and hands is called Kumi Uchi. These are the same methods as the Torite Techniques. That being said there is a single way of thinking with regards to these. A person wearing Tabi will not injure his feet, a barefoot person will hurt his feet.

A mounted rider should be pulled from his horse while a foot soldier should be grabbed by the head and pulled down onto his back. A helmeted warrior should be pulled facedown. A shirtless many should be struck in the chest and the most important thing is to take the enemy's sword. Further, take great care that your own blade is not stolen away. This is a technique that holds or wraps up with the left hand while the right does the action.

の者どもが物見をするに敵の様をうかゞひて見とゞけたる者は治定すべし
たとへば武者の体をみてはかるべし左の手を捨て右の手を遣ひて
抜てもるゝ様を見て戦ひ戦場の法あるを知の事、
他の出陣立て並の事をすゝむるとも其の勢ひを見て考へてよく
する上にあるものを見はかる所にある者を見ぶるを備へに寄て其備
の懸り引にて勝る事を馬上の時は太刀持て敵のかゝりを敵の先に向かふ事
地を知敵の有無に敵の様子を知るべし又目付を以て敵ちかき時は地引の
利をもって進みてもよしされど太刀持て敵少しの時は乱をとる
手なみにして敵として大刀をとりて戦ふ時は乗るをもってするなり

In addition, there is a way to fight whilst holding a sword. Typically an illustration of this extreme situation should be placed here in my opinion but as it is the same I will just write a description.

For a warrior on horseback, cut at the horse. For a man on the ground, trace a circle around him on your horseback and win with Suigetsu no Kurai.

For situations where both are mounted on horseback. If the opponent is holding a Tachi, attack from the opponents left. An opponent holding a spear should be met on the right. These attacking methods are essential.

Further, in the case where you are both armed with the same weapon, it is important to make use of Chi no Ri, or the advantage of the terrain, to your best advantage. In addition, when Muto, or without a sword, and facing off against an enemy the most important thing is Kisen wo Sei Suru 機先を制する, or take the advantage by striking first in an unexpected manner. From there you should next completely block the movement of the enemy's sword and take his weapon away from him.

▲がんせきならびきのこと

此まきもの図面図め此挽くしてよを復きて縫包裹て

跡を待ち来まちたん二ところの内乃老代とおに入る家

おつくる其家まで臈でみわろて到たつある

がんせきくだきの事
Gansekikudaki no Koto
Crushing a Great Rock

The weighted portion of this is formed from a hundred Monme 匁, or 375 grams, of lead. Form it into a ball and cover it with skin. Sew up the seam where the two ends of the hide overlap and attach a short cord. An opponent can be struck between the eyebrows from between two and three Ken, or 3.6 to 5.4 meters/yards away. In the summer or other warmer times striking the chest bone will immediately cause a man to crumple.

	この土はに入れて持ち運ぶ事 You should place this ball in your Tamoto 袂, or sleeve, and carry it about with you.

(Written inside the circle) You should place this ball in your Tamoto 袂, or sleeve, and carry it about with you.
The Sakurai scroll contains the following:
You absolutely cannot use this technique without the express permission of your lord.
This document is a military strategy scroll based on what was revealed by Kusunoki Masashige. It is a secret military document. For further information please refer to the Heihoki.

In the end, the learning of Kenjutsu and Jujutsu are by order of the lord. All of the rest of your studies should be concerned with guarding your principals. Of essence is that you maintain both discretion and a straightforward mindset.
Rather than learning Kenjutsu and then proceeding to travel down a mountain road frequented by bandits you should not take up the study of Kenjutsu and stay afraid of such roads. Thus you will stay safe. You should not forget that there is a Kotowaza 諺, or saying that goes, Nama Byoho wa Okega no Moto 生兵法は大怪我の元. A little bit of military learning will only result in big injuries.

▲手縄の事

はや縄といふハ人をおさへてはやく縄をかけるむすびの入用也其むすびは引かけからげる所の縄を手にてまきさし縄のごとくむすぶ又大事を犯す科人をとらゆる又ハ召捕とも称る也

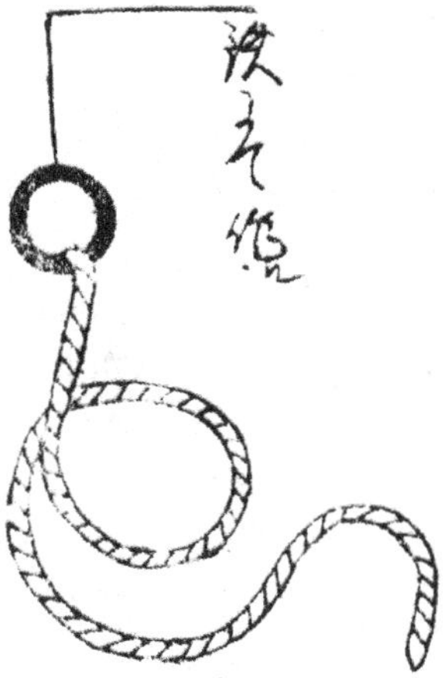

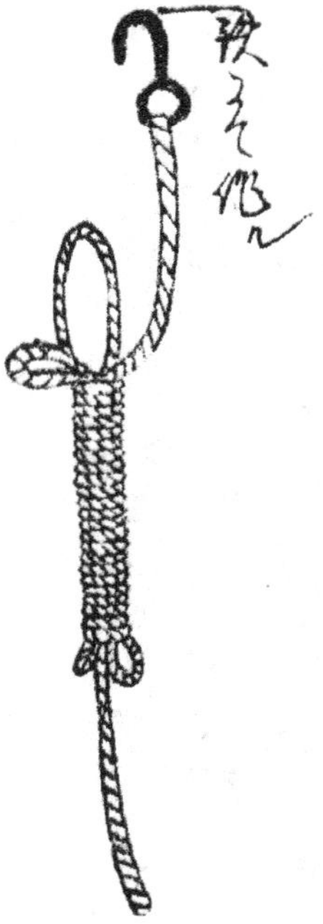

右たゞ結ぶ口伝あり

の事
Hayanawa no Koto
Fast Tie Binding

Hayanawa refers to a method for quickly restraining a person by rapidly tying them up with rope. Typically a long thick rope of Five Shaku, or 1.5 meters is used. On the end of that a hook is attached. A ring is also sometimes used.
There is a Kuden related bringing the rope in to the right.

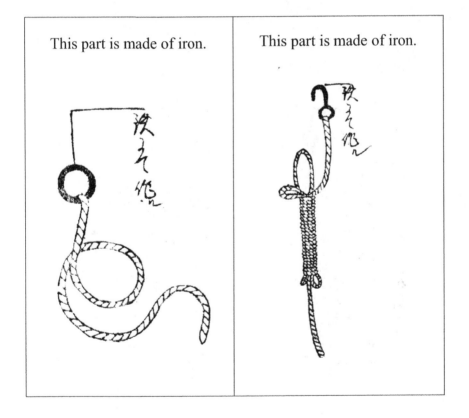

This part is made of iron. 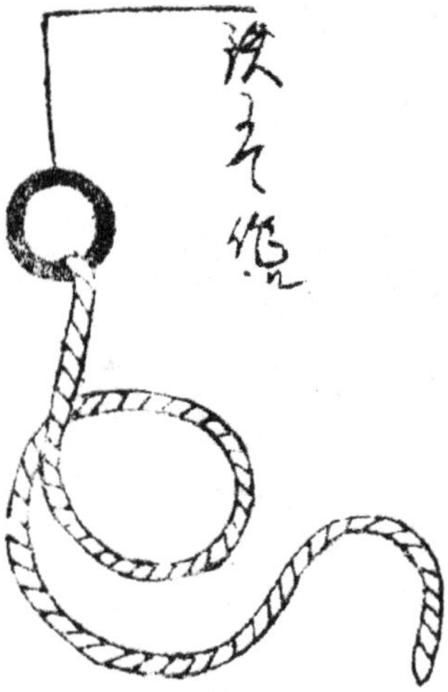	This part is made of iron. 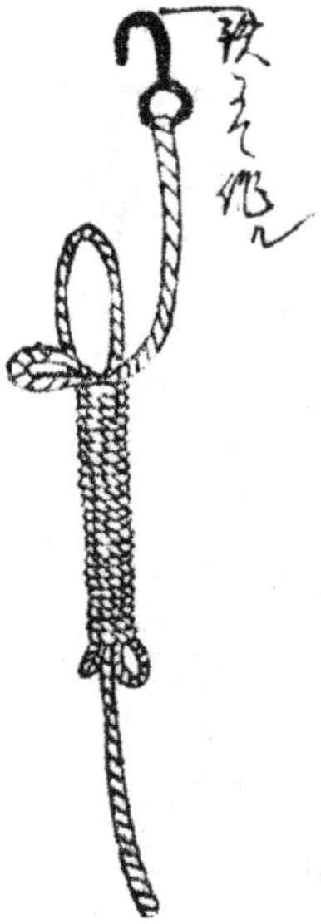

▲九籠出に口伝ある事

九籠出あらば先を残すべし待は時節をもつて勝べき也
下部は時節をもつて勝べき也

▲鑓術虚実の事

凡鑓術の虚実といふは上段を打んと見せて下段をうち下段
を見せて中段をうつとし口伝にて敵をうちまどはす事也
急に来る敵はひらいて討べし緩やかに来る敵は中段の構へ
置しるべし　但敵の眼中を見る事肝要也

▲薬術あて前の事

凡薬術といふは敵の手足を遂に付べし又あて前といふは
の事にて猶強あて又ひとつ長眼の目付にて下をば陰の構
其の位は見しと志るべし

取籠者に心得すること
Torikomori Mono ni Kokoroe suru Koto
How to Handle a Samurai You Have Surrounded

If you have surrounded a person, the first thing you should do in find out who they are. If the person is a Bushi, or Samurai, they will become stronger as time passes. If it is a person of lower status however they will become weaker as time passes.

剣術の事
Kenjutsu Kyojitsu no Koto
Using Truth and Falsehood With the Sword

For the most part within Kenjutsu, the sword arts, the term Kyo-Jitsu, or Truth-Falsehood refer to showing that you are going to cut in from Jodan when you actually are going to cut from Gedan. Show that you are going to cut from Gedan and then cut in from Chudan. It is of the upmost importance to keep this concept in mind as you go into Kamae with the Tachi.

For an opponent that enters quickly, you should open up to one side and strike. For an opponent that attacks slowly it is best to go into Chudan. That being said it is important to watch the opponent's eyes.

A person whose eyes are red (signifying a person who is wound up) should be handled calmly. However a person whose eyes are white (a brave warrior) should be dealt with using sudden violent attacks.

柔術、Error!の事
Jujutsu Atemi no Koto
On the Subject of Jujutsu and Atemi, or Striking

For the most part Jujutsu refers to using a joint lock on the opponent's feet or legs. Further, Atemi striking refers to striking the chest or the area under the armpits. Also striking between the eyes. Below that are points like Kage no Fu, the solar plexus, which if struck is something that cannot be endured.

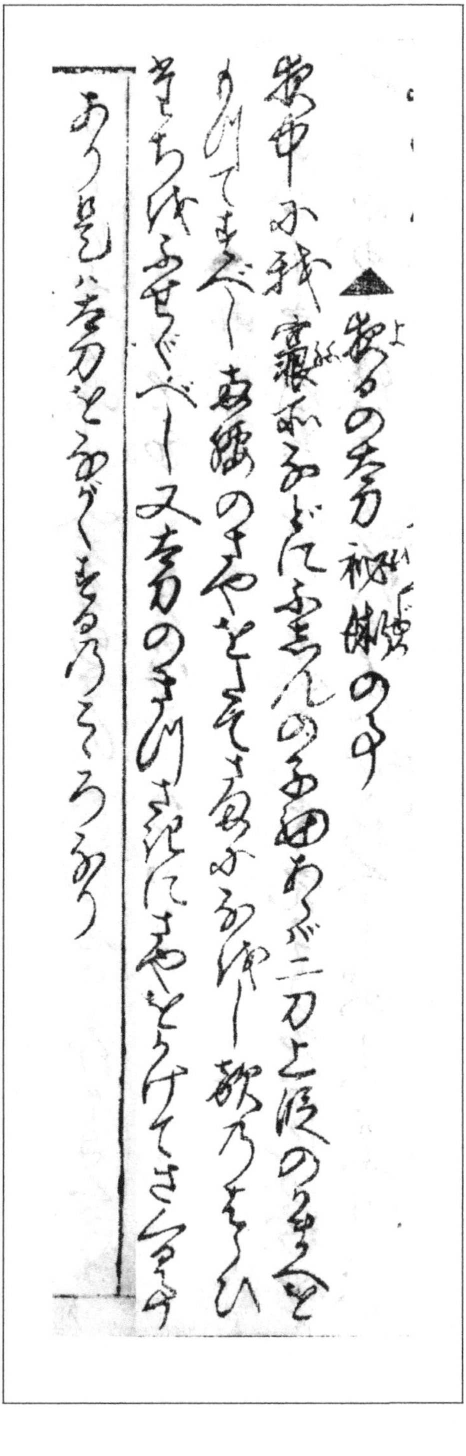

夜の太刀、秘術の事
Yoru no Tachi Hijutsu no Koto
The Secret Technique of Sword Fighting at Night

If you are in your bedroom in the middle of the night and you detect something suspicious, then you should go into Daijodan with your Tachi. Turn the Saya, or scabbard, so it is straight up and down, which will protect you from a waist level cut from the opponent. Further, you can also place the Saya on the end of the sword. You should keep in mind that the feet should be used to maximize the length of the Tachi.

▲眼つかひの事

まなこにかし定法あり身をとゝのへるを定まり庭にしの形を
へて目にかし候とあられけれて合点あるべし敵の心の働を
付つる又其心とも心得ずはさゝに斃るを知りて万事に心づ
かるをひとつとなりて気をの中に入て敵に詰かけて仕
様へいゝよりは居るさしみえるにて其師範に習せて其のことく
去者ハ山中動物があくるまゝ猿猴の様に走るにてこれハ兵
法にはみえあるべし畢竟変化も其者のかしハ稽古を
するの修行をあれハ心法至極の理をか肝要なるべし変化
と知て習熟の所に身を通して万人の変化をもとめて成る
ところ勝負にして心をあかる勝負にしるべし誠にかく兵法の大成
の基としてかけひしとあるべからず

しの事

Metsubushi no Koto

On the Topic of Metsubushi, Blinding powders

Open a small hole in an egg's shell. Blow out the contents and fill it with powdered Togarashi, or red pepper, and cover the hole with paper. Then put it in your Tamoto, or end of the sleeve of your Kimono. When you are faced with an enemy smash it on their face. Also you can bury a poisonous Mamushi snake in the ground and pile horse manure on top. Add finely chopped grass and mix it. After powdering it, roll it in paper tissue like you would use to wipe your nose. Blowing it at an opponent will cause them to lose consciousness. This method is rather incomplete and has not been fully tested. You should probably rely more on the teachings of your master and not attempt it without his permission. This is but an extract of the Record of Military Strategy left to us by Yamamoto Kansuke.

In the end it is essential to understand that both Kenjutsu and Jujutsu are not only to protect the life of your lord but are tools with which you can protect yourself and keep yourself on the correct path. Despite knowing Kenjutsu it is best to err on the side of caution and not enter a mountain road infested with brigands. There is a saying that goes "A little bit of military training can be the cause of great injury."

軍法兵法記　奥義巻

一

▲敵二人我一人仕合之事

夫敵ハ二人我ハ一人ニて仕合ときハ二人のてきを向ふうけて右の方れ敵へかゝる氣色をよこさせて左の敵へ立廻るべし右の方れ敵後へ廻らんとせバわきへひらきて左のさの敵を撃べし

軍法兵法記・奥義の巻

Record of Military Strategy and Soldiering
Ogi no Maki - The Inner Secrets Scroll

敵二人、我一人試合の事
Teki Futari, Ware Hitori Shiai no Koto
When You Are Alone Against Two Attackers

The learning of Kenjutsu and Jujutsu are by the order of the lord however all other study should be devoted to keeping yourself on the true path and preserving your integrity. This is very important.

When you are alone and facing two opponents, position yourself so you are standing opposite both of them. Give the impression that you are going to attack the opponent on your right, then join combat with the enemy on your left.

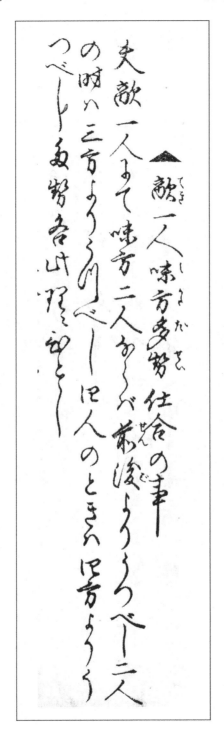

▲敵一人味方多勢仕合の事

夫敵一人にて味方二人ならば前後よりうつべし二人の時ハ三方よりうつべし四人のときハ四方よりうつべし多勢各此理を知べし

敵一人、味方多数試合の事

Teki Hitori, Mikata Tasu Shiai no Koto

Fighting Against One Person With Many Soldiers

If there is but a single enemy soldier and two of your warriors, one of you should attack from behind. If there are three of you then strike in from three different directions. If there are four of you attack from four different directions. For greater numbers follow this same principal.

▲川中仕合之事

夫川中まて歩立の仕合ハ敵を川よりおきまれへてきの方下をしかひよ立向べし其理ハ其一ハあらくこむかへハ陽性をうくる理其二ハ川より流るゝ物の穢をうけざる理あるを以なり

▲又の子ち小あい

川中試合の事
Kawanaka Shiai no Koto
Fighting in the Middle of a River

When fighting a battle in a river you should position your forces so that the enemy is upstream from you. You should be on the right-hand side, diagonally opposite the enemy. The underlying theory here is, first of all, if you are facing the flow of the river you can receive the Yosei 陽性, or combined energy of the opponent and the river. Second, scraps of wood and so forth that flow down from upstream will not cause a damage to your forces.

If during the afternoon the sunlight should be to your back. If you are armed with Yari 鑓, or spears, then your forces should be placed at the Mizu-giwa 水際, or where the water meets the land. They should strike from Gedan Kamae. This will help to conserve your energy.

▲家内仕合の事

夫家内にて仕合よくば先敵にて安きをしるべし 凶と
勝負と難所と工夫して家ハ助勢に居て敵をなん所
に定べし 又おのれが家内よりしてハ時刻をのぞむべし
他の家内にして即時に勝をとるべし

▲日中仕合の事

夫日中に仕合ときハ日を背に受べし 気塞りなる利有
又敵を日に向はすれバ目まぎれして我が勝めをとるもの
なり

▲月影仕合の事

夫月影に仕合ときハ我ハ陰の方に居て敵を月に
向はすべし 其のまぎれて敵をあつかはしむるの
利有なり

試合の事
Kanai Shiai no Koto
Fighting in a House

Should you ever have to join combat within a house you should first gauge the height of the ceiling as well as the distance to the walls on your right and left. Next, you should consider your Joyo 助用 or the spot which is the most advantageous for you, in addition to your Nansho 難所, or your weak point in the room. Devise a Kufu, or device, that will allow you to be set up in the beneficial Joyo position. At the same time the enemy should be forced into the most difficult position, the Nansho.

Further, if you are within your own home try to delay the confrontation as much as possible. Should you be in a dwelling not your own then try to end the confrontation as quickly as possible.

試合の事
Nicchu Shiai no Koto
Fighting During Midday

When fighting during the day be sure to have the sun at your back. You will receive a beneficial push of Ki 気 or spirit. Further, the sun will be bright in the enemy's eyes and they will not be able to read the faces of your men.

試合の事
Tukiyo Shiai no Koto
Fighting on a Moonlit Night

When fighting at night under a moon lit sky, you should place your forces in the shadow and the moonlight in the enemy's face. The benefit is that you will be hidden and the faces of the enemy will be clearly illuminated.

▲指物仕合之事

夫さしものゝ仕合といふハ身をはなれて敵のうち

をとらるゝをうし紛怒れいろをとるべし身難所にあ

らば我まへ小敵て仕合をきなすり

▲敵我後来被事

夫敵我後ゟりきたりて云をうけとらんとせば

ときハ右の方ゟむくきて利あるなり

試合の事

Yamiyo Shiai no Koto

Fighting on a Dark Night

When battling on a dark night drop your body down low and concentrate on the formation the enemy has taken and try to determine how they are armed. Note however that should the terrain not be to your advantage you should move in and engage the enemy.

It can be beneficial to conceal your forces in a dark place in order to spy on the enemy.

敵が後方から来た時、く事

Teki ga Koho Kara Kita Toki, Hiraku Koto

Opening up When Attacked From Behind

If an enemy approaches from behind and calls out to you as he cuts in, the best defense is to move out to the right. This will all be to the enemy's disadvantage.

▲敵顔色氣指見る事

丈斬合仕合の時ニ当て敵の氣色をみるにおゐて
なるへし性氣上るいきほひなり性氣のよはる則は
勝利工夫ある事も多くむつかしくなるものなり
次ニ氣色悪向なるハ心底ある謂なり心かくある
ときは命をおしむものなり命おしむ則は向をさく
なき勝利をとるさまへも遁んすをのみおもふもの
なり故に敵の氣指を見て利をとる事ハ敵ニを
見ると知へしをきとをもつると知り下をみるときは
逃るとをもるへし知なり

敵顔色顔持見る事
Teki Kao Iro Kao Mochi Miru Koto
Observing the Enemy's Face

It is important to look at the face of your enemy when you are set to engage in a Kiri-Ai 斬り合い or a sword fight. If the face has become red then the enemy is not in their right mind. As they have become unstrung it is not necessary to resort to a Kufu. Their spirit is not settled.

Next, if the face is pale it is evidence of a person who is fearful. When a person is fearful they value their life greatly and are unlikely to strike first. Such a person is not thinking about winning, only of escaping.

Further, in order to gain an advantage by judging the enemy's face, know that when the opponent is looking up he is observing something in the distance. When looking downward he is observing something nearby. It is important not to Yudan 油断, or become careless or miscalculate here.

◆足場悪地にて仕合之事

夫足場悪き地にて仕合之ハ刀をとりまはしとしての剣を
ちらうすべし 若又前ハ足場あしくして後へあしべ 緩く
あしくバ我先足場あしき地を取て時に而て我ハ足場
能地に退歌をあしぞあしき地に動へし

にて試合の事

Ashiba Akuchi Ni Te Shiai no Koto

Fighting on Uneven Ground

Should you have to engage in combat in a place where the footing is poor, first of all it is best not to move your body around. You should also consider how you can use the situation to your advantage. For example, if the footing is bad on the ground in front of you and behind you it is good, place yourself in the area of bad footing. When the enemy makes their way over to you move to the more solid ground thereby placing the enemy forces on bad footing.

A Quick Guide to Martial Arts

End

Made in the USA
Coppell, TX
04 November 2020

40776910R00085